Wonderplay

Interactive & Developmental Games, Crafts, & Creative Activities for Infants, Toddlers, & Preschoolers

From the 92nd St. Y Parenting Center

By Fretta Reitzes & Beth Teitelman, with Lois Alter Mark
Illustrated by Paul Kepple

RUNNING PRESS
PHILADELPHIA · LONDON

9 8 7 6 5
Digit on the right indicates the number of this printing.

Library of Congress Cataloging-in-Publication Number
94–67769

ISBN 1–56138–575–1

Cover and interior design and illustrations
by Paul Kepple
Interior photography courtesy of the 92nd St. Y.
Typeset in Vag Rounded and Courier

Permissions: "A Rum Sum Sum," from **The Great
Rounds Songbook**, by Esther Nelson, Copyright © 1985
by Sterling Publishing Co., Reprinted by permission.
"The Bumble Bee," by Mrs. Nancy Takerer, Reprinted
by permission. "The Dressing Song," by Fretta Reitzes,
Reprinted by permission. "Funny Bunny Song," by
Rebecca Kwawer, Reprinted by permission. "Head,
Shoulders, Knees, and Toes," "If You're Happy and You
Know It," and "Itsy-Bitsy Spider," from **It's Toddler Time**,
Copyright © 1982 by Kimbo Educational, Long Branch,
NJ., Reprinted by permission. "I'm a Little Baby," by
Anna Kwawer, Reprinted by permission. "Little Red
Caboose," from **The Cokesbury Game Book**, by
Arthur M. Depew, Copyright © 1960 by Abingdon
Press, Reprinted by permission. "Little Red Wagon,"
by Luigi Creatore and Hugo Peretti, Copyright ©
1957 (Renewed) by Music Sales Corporation (ASCAP),
Reprinted by permission, International copyright
secured, All rights reserved. "Monkey See, Monkey
Do," by Tina Harris and Kevin Alan O'Neal, Copyright
© 1989 by Showthem Sounds, Garson Music, AMH
Kidd, Harrindur Publishing Co., Reprinted by permis-
sion. "Sky Song," by Timothy Reitzes, Reprinted by
permission. "Swing Song," by Alexandra Reitzes,
Reprinted by permission. "Three Little Monkeys,"
Copyright © 1956 by Creston Music Co. (Renewed),
Reprinted by permission, All rights reserved.

This book may be ordered by mail from the publisher.
Please add $2.50 for postage and handling.
But try your bookstore first!

Running Press Book Publishers
125 South Twenty-second Street
Philadelphia, Pennsylvania 19103–4399

**A WORD OF CAUTION: As you do the activities
described in this book, please use good judgment
and common sense, and always keep safety in mind.
The authors and publishers of this book have no
responsibility for any unintended or improper applica-
tion of any of the suggestions in this book.**

For Jack, Ali, and Tim–F.R.
For Jay, Rebecca, and Anna–B.T.
For Michael, Alex, Sara, and Sophie–L.A.M.

Contents

94 Moving Up in the World Three-Year-Olds

Introduction

Welcome to the 92nd Street Y Parenting Center. Back in the spring of 1979, there were few resources available for parents. Support groups, books, and magazines for parents were limited. Child development experts were not commonly seen in newspapers and on television, and organized classes and activities for very young children were just getting started. It was then that the 92nd Street YM-YWHA first opened its new "Center for Parents." The Center offered a variety of play groups, seminars, and events, as well as a drop-in resource room for parents and their children. Our aim was to offer the opportunity for parents to make friends, share experiences, and gain confidence as their children grew up.

The response was overwhelming. Surrounded by parents, babies, strollers, and toys, we realized that there was a genuine need for these programs. The 92nd Street Y was already an old and trusted community and cultural center that had served its users for more than 100 years—parents trusted the Y and knew that this new Parenting Center would continue the Y's commitment to quality. The Parenting Center grew dramatically.

Since then, through many changes in family life, the Parenting Center has developed innovative programs for parents and children. Thousands of families have participated, and organizations nationwide and from abroad continue to visit us as they develop similar programs in their own communities.

Now, WONDERPLAY brings the Parenting Center directly to you. All the activities in this book can be enjoyed in your living room, kitchen, or backyard, using everyday items you already have on hand and a few inexpensive, easy-to-find additions. Full of ideas, recipes, songs, projects, make-believe games, and practical tips, WONDERPLAY takes parents and children from infancy through the preschool years. You will learn how to choose age-appropriate activities and materials and how to think creatively about playing with your child.

Use WONDERPLAY to spark your imagination. Pick and choose what fits the moment and have a great time playing together. Beach balls, cardboard boxes, paper towel rolls, bubbles, and sponges will never look the same to you again.

Safe and Happy Play

Before you begin using the activities in this book, take some time to think about doing them safely. Be sure to babyproof and toddlerproof your home so that you have a safe and secure play environment.

Each section spans a wide age range. Although these suggestions are offered enthusiastically, none of them is essential at a particular age. Consider YOUR child's developmental readiness and wait until your child is safely able to handle a particular activity. Don't push your child to participate in an activity that is beyond his or her physical ability. NEVER LEAVE YOUR CHILD UNATTENDED.

Ask your pediatrician or nurse-practitioner all questions about your child's physical activity and motor development. Their expertise should be your guide. Be sure to scale movements and activities to your baby's or toddler's size and remember not to play on high surfaces such as beds and changing tables. When you use the floor, make sure that it is well-padded or cushioned.

Check the labels on the paint, glue, and other art materials you use to ensure that they are non-toxic and safe. Always stay with your child when art materials, water, sand, or bubbles are being used. Always keep scissors out of your child's reach and reserve them for adult use only.

When cooking with your child, don't use sharp instruments or utensils, or breakable containers. Keep electrical appliances out of reach and exclude any ingredients to which your child may be allergic. The oven and stove-top are for adult use only.

When playing outdoors, check all areas for potentially hazardous materials such as broken glass, poisonous plants, or animal traces. Supervise your child at all times and wash your hands thoroughly afterward.

Common sense and caution will go a long way toward helping you to enjoy your playtime together.

Sam
three and ½ years

Keisha
three years

Shelly
seven months

Arthur
two years

Bobby
three years

tad
eight months

Chuck
three years

The Y's of it All

Play with Children of All Ages

Daisy
one year

MOLLY
three weeks

Meilo
three and ½ years

Mike
two years

Jim
one year

The Y's of it All
Play with Children of All Ages

Highs and lows are all part of the natural land-scape of everyday life with young children. Babies, toddlers, and preschoolers are all lovable and funny as they amaze you with their growth and development. These years are full of exciting milestones—the first smile, the first steps, the first words, and that magical moment when they climb to the top of the slide on their own.

But children are also demanding, exhausting, and unpredictable. They need you all day long—to get them a snack, to tie their shoelaces, to give them a bath, to keep them safe, and to help when things don't go their way. After all, it will be a long time until they have the physical skills and emotional resources they will need to negotiate the world on their own. All you do with them and for them during these early years will make it possible for them to become independent and competent later on.

"The Y's of It All" is a collection of ideas, suggestions, and practical tips that you can adapt to your own family, whatever the age of your children. With a little bit of thought and a trick or two up your sleeve, you can ride out some of the highs and lows while having a good time along the way.

Special Spaces

A little imagination can turn familiar territory into an exciting new place for your child. These special spaces give your child a sense of privacy, ownership, and a setting for imaginative play. Look for small, cozy places, like a tight corner, or under a desk. Children might enjoy bringing several toys and perhaps a snack on their visit to this new favorite spot. And don't forget to bring your flashlight!

For indoor play, turn an old bathroom rug into a magic carpet. Throw a sheet over a table to make a house. Drape a towel between two chairs for a secret hiding place. For a more permanent special space, use heavy tape to stretch a sheet or large piece of fabric between two walls—a hallway works perfectly. Keep this sheet up for a few days so it's available in the morning when your child is ready to play.

You can also make special spaces outdoors. Throw a towel over two tall bushes that have a nice, usable space in-between. Lean a sheet of corrugated cardboard from a large carton against a tree for a great, child-sized sitting spot.

These homemade special spaces are great places for your child to play, either alone or with a friend.

Local Trips

A trip doesn't have to include a ticket, a suitcase, and an airplane. Young children can find even a trip around the corner exciting. Take a local excursion to someplace new or familiar for the sheer pleasure of exploring a destination. These outings are not to accomplish errands or chores, but rather for the simple fun and enjoyment of going someplace special.

The things adults see and take for granted every day can be new and interesting to a child. Through their eyes, nails of many different shapes in the hardware store or the variety of fish in the pet store can be fascinating. Think about what your neighborhood or local area offers. Could you visit a firehouse, college campus, library, airport, bank, post office, farm, lumberyard, or even a special tree or garden down the block? Even a short trip to nowhere on a public bus or train can be great fun.

Play along with your child's sense of adventure. Pack a small travel bag with a snack or favorite toy. Look for "souvenirs"—train tickets, bank deposit slips, or post office forms.

Bon voyage!

Bedtime

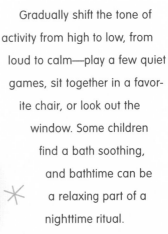

With the end of each day comes bedtime. Sometimes it will be easy for your child to say "good night" and go to bed. You'll enjoy these evenings. Other nights your child will have a hard time making the transition from daytime activity to sleep. After all, saying "good night" means being away from you and all that they love to do until the next morning. These nights are hard for everyone.

Although there's no one way to handle bedtime, it's worth making an effort to develop an evening routine and a bedtime ritual that works for your family. This part of the day can be pleasurable, as well.

Begin by deciding when bedtime will be, based on your child's sleep patterns and daily rhythms. Leave enough time for a smooth transition so that your child will know what to expect.

Gradually shift the tone of activity from high to low, from loud to calm—play a few quiet games, sit together in a favorite chair, or look out the window. Some children find a bath soothing, and bathtime can be a relaxing part of a nighttime ritual.

Bedtime stories are a traditional favorite. Make up a story or read a book. If the number of stories keeps growing, set a limit that's the same every night. With a young baby, lower the lights, sing some quiet songs, or rock and walk together. The goal is to have a predictable and satisfying routine that leads to saying "good night."

Respect your child's individual needs for a favorite stuffed animal or a blanket to sleep with. These beloved objects help children say "good night" more easily. Children may find a small nightlight, lamp, or hall light comforting. Soft music sometimes helps, as does leaving the door open.

YAWN

But some nights will be difficult. From time to time, you may need to change routines that once worked—your child may need more or less sleep. At times it will be hard for them to separate from you. There may be tears and protests, you may experience uncertainty about picking up your baby, and you may make repeated trips back to the bedroom. Learning to go to sleep on your own takes a long time. Be patient.

Choosing a Good Book

You and your child will look at books together for many years ahead, and you'll find favorites that become special to you both. When choosing a book for your child, find one that appeals to you as well. You'll be reading the book over and over, and if you enjoy it, reading together will become a pleasurable time for you both.

Look for books with clear pictures or photographs that your child can recognize. Children love to hear about everyday happenings that reflect their own experiences. Also look for stories with children or animals as main characters.

If a book is too long, your child will let you know. Try to tell a shortened version in your own words. Or save it for later years when your child is ready for the full version.

Look for books with dramatic sound effects to read—animals, traffic, or instruments. Read them with gusto, and your child will enjoy your enthusiasm and imitate you. It's fun to read dramatically, so embellish the text with sound effects and use a variety of character voices to make a story come alive.

Obtain books your child can hold and handle alone. Board books are especially good for babies and young toddlers. You can wipe them off, and they can even withstand a bite or two. Children love pop-up and lift-the-flap books, but these books are fragile, so when you buy these books, expect to use tape to keep them in good working order. As your child gets older, you'll move on to a wonderful selection of picture storybooks available in both libraries and bookstores.

Young babies and toddlers may look at a book with you for quite a long time, and they may enjoy the cozy feeling of being close to you. But at times they may not. Accept their level of interest at any given moment and look forward to times when they are more ready to share the pleasure of being read to. They will bring you the book and crawl into your lap, and "Read me a story" will become music to your ears.

Playing Together and Sharing

Getting together with friends—at your house or theirs—can be great fun for your children. Playing together and learning to share are important parts of life, but it takes children a long time to do this successfully. There are many ups and downs along the way. Both children may want the same toy at the same time, and they are too young to take turns. Your visitor may want to use the new truck your child just received for a birthday. Both children may dissolve into tears for no apparent reason. However, there are ways to help your child through this process.

If playtime is at your home, let your child choose a few special items that don't have to be shared. Put them in the closet to avoid problems. Let your child choose a few toys that will be shared with friends.

If you're the visitor, have your child bring a toy or two along. This way, the sharing won't be one-sided and each child has something to offer.

Plan a few neutral activities that don't involve one child's toys. Make a snack, play with play dough, dance to music, or chase bubbles—all good ways for children to have fun together. Going outside for a change of scene also helps.

But no matter how well you prepare, disputes over toys are inevitable. Expect them and help your child at those rough times. One technique that works with some children over two is to use a kitchen timer to time turns. Set it for short, toddler-sized times so no one waits too long. A timer can turn a dispute into a new game.

Try to plan visits to accommodate both children's schedules and avoid naptime or cranky hours. Keep visits short. When you see their good moods giving way, tell them that playtime will end in five more minutes. Children often need transition time to finish what they're doing and get ready to move on.

Cleaning up together is important. Together, children and parents can put toys in a big bag or box to sort out later. This final activity puts closure on the visit.

With experience, good times with friends, and lots of patience on your part, playing together and sharing will become a satisfying part of your child's life.

19

Bathtime as Playtime

The "no-purpose bath" is a terrific activity that two- and three-year-olds really enjoy, especially on a hot summer day. This is a bath just for the fun of it and has nothing to do with getting clean. You don't need any soap—although all the ideas that follow work with a real bath, too! Get ready for a good time, but make sure everything you need is on hand to avoid leaving your child alone in the bathroom.

Try seating your child in the tub before it's filled so he can feel the stream of water as it enters. Children love to feel the rush of water coming out of the spout, and to hold a bucket under it. Older children can blow bubbles in the water through bendable straws.

There are lots of objects you'll find around the house that will make bathtime a much-anticipated event. Plastic containers, pitchers, and scoops are ideal bath toys. Poke holes in margarine tubs so children can make it "rain," use soap dishes as boats, and let children "paint" the tiles with a housepainting brush dipped in water. Be sure to bring plastic funnels and strainers, too.

Open a package of clean sponges so your child can wipe the tiles. Washcloths are also easy bath toys, and they're wonderful peek-a-boo toys for babies. Toddlers and preschoolers enjoy watching a washcloth billow, laying it on top of the water, and observing the patterns as it gets wet.

Assemble a collection of inexpensive rubber ducks, boats, and dolls that are made especially for the bath. Make sure your child understands that there are special toys for the bath, and that not everything can go into the tub.

Keep all your bathtime paraphernalia in a net bag that allows the toys to drip dry. Give them a good washing every once in a while to avoid mold and mildew.

Bathtime is a wonderful opportunity for your child to learn about his or her body. Ask your child to put one finger of soap on a toe, on his or her nose, or on his or her belly button.

Bathtime can also be a nice, intimate time to be with your child. While in the bath, children will often relax, sing, and chatter while you just listen and enjoy being with them.

Birthdays

Children love to feel special, and that's what a birthday is all about. Although at young ages children are not yet able to understand the concept of a birthday, by two or three years old they look forward to this extraordinary day.

There are many ways to celebrate a young child's birthday, but big celebrations are often overwhelming, so be sensitive to what your child can manage. Even with a small, child-sized party, children may become overexcited or fall apart. If this happens, take a little time out to calm down and comfort your child so he can go on with the day.

Keep celebrations short and simple. Invite two or three playmates and their parents for an hour or so to play and celebrate together. Instead, you may want to have a small family party. Either way, children look forward to the cake, the candles, and singing "Happy Birthday." For the birthday child, being sung to, hearing his or her name, and blowing out the candles can be the highlight of the party.

Here are a few suggestions: Consider giving a cupcake to each child. They help every guest to feel as if they have a cake of their own.

You can keep party bags simple as well— it's not necessary to fill them with all kinds of toys. Little children are thrilled to get anything— a box of crayons, a small drawing pad, or a container of bubbles.

Too many new things at once can be overwhelming for a young child, and too much to take in at one time. You can put some unopened presents away to open later, after everyone goes home, and "after party letdown" sets in. Or save some for another day, when all the birthday excitement has passed.

There are many things you can do together to enjoy this day. Decorate a Happy Birthday sign with your child's name. Make a paper crown to wear. Decorate the cake with sprinkles or animal crackers, and make the day last longer by taking pictures to look at together until the next birthday.

Dressing Up

Very young children love to dress up in adult clothing and costumes. It's delightful to see your toddler wearing your shoes and hat, marching through the house, imitating your every word. A dress-up box accessible to your child can provide some wonderful and satisfying playtimes. Keep on hand old purses, hats, adult-sized shirts and shoes, scarves to tie around the waist, and old costume jewelry. The best costumes are usually the ones you make yourself, so add paper crowns, or make capes by attaching strings to old towels.

As your children move into the world of dramatic play, you can provide props for their inspiration: a yard or two of tulle from the fabric shop, feather boas, a toy firefighter's hat, or a pair of plastic sunglasses. Your child will take it from there.

Consider having doubles of some costume items to use when friends come over. Dressing up is a wonderful outlet for playing together.

Welcome the new cast of characters who will suddenly appear—kings, queens, astronauts, superheroes, mommies, and daddies.

Found Objects

Found objects are things we have all around us in our daily lives. We use them and throw them out. However, these items offer your child a stockpile of materials for creative activities. Milk cartons turn into building blocks. Oatmeal boxes become drums. Add scissors, tape, glue, and paints, and you and your child can be artists, builders, and designers together.

Keep on hand a box filled with many of these items, so you always have something from which to choose. And keep your eyes open for anything new and interesting to add.

Grocery store standards:

detergent cups • egg cartons • milk cartons • paper towel rolls • plastic food containers • plastic fruit trays • plastic soda bottles • toilet paper rolls

Fabric store basics:

fabric swatches • felt • large buttons • spools • yarn

Packing materials:

ribbons • tissue paper • wrapping paper scraps

Miscellaneous materials:

cardboard and cardboard boxes • color strips from the paint store • magazines and children's catalogs (pre-cut some pictures, keep some whole) • wallpaper samples

Nature

Children are very curious about the natural world around them—even a walk around the block can take an hour with a two-year-old! Children often stop to smell the roses, feel the breeze, or watch an earthworm crawl.

Nurturing a child's inborn curiosity encourages learning about the natural world. Your child may become fascinated by a ladybug. Take as long as your child wants to examine it. Watch it walk across a hand. Count its dots. Talk about its colors. It's not necessary to become an expert on ladybugs, with complex explanations. Offer simple, basic answers to your child's questions, and when you don't know the answer, say so.

Children learn through active use of all their senses. Pulling a petal off a flower is a way to feel its texture and to discover how a flower is put together. Children love to feel mud, sand, and water. They love to listen to ducks, crickets, and the sounds of rain. You may want a book from the library for another look at the things you've seen.

Children are particularly observant of changes. Leaves turning color, flowers fading, and puddles disappearing fascinate them. Stop, look, and listen together as you rediscover the natural world through the eyes of your child.

Holidays

Every year has its round of holidays and celebrations to anticipate and to prepare for. But holiday celebrations can bring changes in your daily routine with babies and very young children. Sometimes travel, new people, new places to sleep, different mealtimes, and later bedtimes may have to be adapted to your child's needs.

Think ahead and try to anticipate that some changes might be difficult for your child. If you are traveling, try to get the information you need to plan. Where will your baby nap? Where can you spend much-needed quiet time with your toddler? What can you tell your three-year-old about where he or she will be sleeping? Preparing in advance can make the entire holiday more enjoyable for both you and your child.

Holiday celebrations often include relatives and friends who are new to your child. Some babies and children enjoy being passed around and introduced to many people at one time. Others don't. Be available for your child. Try to recognize when they have had enough celebration and socializing.

As your children grow, look for ways to include them in the celebration. They may like to create something special for the table, decorate menus or placecards, make the wrapping paper or help with the cooking. Holidays can be wonderful times to create family rituals. Children love traditions and look forward to being part of them. And taking pictures of your children at these special times can provide a wonderful record through the years.

Most of all, remember that if your children see you enjoying the holidays, chances are they'll enjoy them, too. You will look back on these occasions as good family time together.

The Rainy Day Box

Days with toddlers and preschoolers can seem long sometimes. There are many hours to fill, especially if the weather is bad or your child is sick. It's fun to have a "Rainy Day Box" full of surprises for these occasions. Something fresh and different brings new energy to your day.

Here are some ideas for a Rainy Day Box: Include art supplies such as new paintbrushes, a fresh drawing pad, unusual markers, a package of stickers, or a container of play dough. Add a new toy, book, or music tape. Secretly put in an unopened birthday present, or something your child hasn't used in a while so you both can take a fresh look at it.

If there's a recipe that you'd like to try with your child, put it away in the box. Add some new cookie cutters or an interesting kitchen utensil. Cooking is great for these occasions. Include musical instruments, or a special dress-up item or prop.

Give your box a special name and dramatize its magical appearance out of nowhere. Decorate it with your child, if you wish. Children love the ceremony of reaching in for a surprise and finding something unexpected. At the end of the day, return your Rainy Day Box to its secret hiding place in your closet. Remember, the box is reserved for you to bring out only when the day seems long.

Car Travel

Car travel with babies and young children can sometimes be difficult, and it's even tempting to stay home to avoid the inevitable upsets. However, there are plenty of activities to keep your child happily distracted while safely sitting in a car seat. A little bit of effort on your part will go a long way toward making your time in the car better for everyone.

Your child can pack a special car bag with small, easy, manageable toys. Keep your own stash of surprises in the car—try an unbreakable mirror and an assortment of funny hats, a color wheel or spinner from a board game, soft hand puppets, or even some bells. Keep on hand a large pad with a firm back, and one or two crayons. Tie the crayons to the pad with a short string so that if it drops, your child can retrieve it. A special surprise envelope with pictures, or a few paint sample color strips provide a novel diversion when the going gets rough. Look at them together and talk about what you see.

Always bring along your child's favorite possession of the moment—a blanket, a doll, a stuffed animal. These will help your child feel content and comfortable in the car and away from home.

If you're sitting in the back seat with your child, books are a great way to pass the time. However, if you're driving, storybook tapes are a lifesaver.

Check the library for them—many of your child's favorite books are now available on audiotape. Replaying your child's favorite story may make your trip easier and more fun.

Singing and clapping games are big hits with babies and toddlers. And remember a favorite, familiar nighttime song to help your baby fall asleep. Of course, if you're doing the driving, you can use musical tapes to entertain your child while you concentrate on the road.

When your child is tall enough to see out the window, you've reached a welcome turning point in car travel! You can now play a variety of games. Who can be the first to spot a stop sign, a truck, or a green car? Take turns naming things you see out the window—"I see a bird in the sky! What do you see?" "I see a garbage truck. What do you see?" As your child gets older, you'll enjoy watching the clouds, counting the cars, and making up your own special brand of family car games.

So gather your things, get in the car, buckle up, and have a great trip!

A Sense of Wonder

Birth to Six Months

A Sense of Wonder
Birth to Six Months

Your newborn baby, although totally dependent on your love and care, begins life ready to emerge as an individual, with a unique personality and temperament. Newborns spend a lot of time eating and sleeping, but they are constantly learning about the world around them, and they become more connected to it every day. They learn quickly to recognize your face and your voice, and eventually know when you are there, making their world safe, secure, and comfortable. And one day soon, your baby smiles at you for the first time. What an incredible moment for you both!

Babies grow quickly. Throughout the first six months, it's fascinating to see your baby master new skills. He discovers his fingers and toes. She reaches and grasps. He holds his head up and looks around. She rocks from side to side, and then rolls over. He pushes himself up and rocks back and forth. She communicates through different cries and sounds. These are all major accomplishments for a very young baby, giving everyone a great feeling of pride and satisfaction.

By playing with your baby during this period of growth, you can learn a lot about your baby's temperament. Infants have different thresholds for physical activity, noise, and stimulation. Some enjoy being rocked, bounced, sung to, and played with endlessly. Others have a greater need for calmer, quieter, shorter playtimes. While one baby may enjoy the normal hubbub of family life, another may find it overwhelming. Take your cue from your baby. Stop when he's had enough, knowing that he'll soon be ready to play again.

Playing with your infant is essential to establishing and strengthening a loving family relationship. In your time together, you will discover the moments when your baby seems ready to play. In this chapter are songs, rhymes, and suggestions for things you can do together during these early playtimes. Keep it simple and have a wonderful time getting to know each other.

Getting Started

Young babies are fairly stationary. However, there are many ways to have fun together as they begin to discover their fingers and toes.

*CUCKOO CLOCK

Babies love to move and sway. Here is a little game for you to play while you are holding your baby on your lap facing you. Sway back and forth, singing,

> **Tick tock, tick tock, I'm a little**
>
> **cuckoo clock.**
>
> **Tick tock, tick tock, now**
>
> **I'm striking one**
>
> **o'clock.**
>
> **CUCKOO!**

If your baby likes this game, go all around the clock together.

*CIRCLE WALK

You hold your baby for many hours during the day, and sometimes a little game can soothe and comfort your baby and help you to pass the time. Walk around in a circle, and add a little song:

> **We're walking in a circle, we're**
>
> **walking in a circle,**
>
> **We're walking in a circle until it's**
>
> **time to stop.**

Then stop, and try, "We're running in a circle." Also try tiptoeing, gliding, and swaying.

During these months, babies "coo." Don't be surprised to find yourself cooing in response. Enjoy these wonderful, early conversations.

*MIRROR DANCING

Babies love to watch "the baby in the mirror," even though they don't yet know who it is! Do some of your walking, holding, and singing in front of the mirror. Watch your baby's expression!

*PEEKABOO GAMES

As your baby begins to recognize you and smile, you can begin to play "Peekaboo." This timeless classic has limitless variations. Anywhere and everywhere, peekaboo games are always possible. There are lots of ways to hide your face. Use your hands, a cloth diaper, a hat, a colorful scarf, or a cute stuffed animal. "Peekaboo, I see you."

*BICYCLING

While your baby is on her back looking up at you, gently move her legs back and forth as if she's riding a bicycle. Add a favorite song for rhythm and fun. For variation, try a scissors motion, moving your baby's legs open and shut. Have a great ride!

around in front of your baby's gazing eyes. You'll find more about bubbles on pages 44 and 76.

✳ RIBBON SHEETS

Ribbon sheets are a homemade item that take a bit of time to make, but are worth the effort. You'll need a collection of differently colored ribbons, each about 18 inches long, and a large piece of fabric. An old receiving blanket will do the trick, but a piece of an old sheet or other fabric is fine as well. If the fabric is thin, double it for strength. Sew one end of each ribbon to the fabric securely, making a row of hanging streamers.

Hold your ribbon sheet above your baby so that the ribbons are within arm's reach. Your baby will enjoy the colorful display as you wave it gently and will begin to bat the ribbons and eventually grab and pull them. Bob it up and down as you sing and talk to your baby.

Save your ribbon sheet as your baby grows. It will become a terrific decoration for a play corner, a great stage curtain for a puppet theater, or a lively costume for dress-up.

✳ RIBBON WASHCLOTH

This is a portable variation on the ribbon sheet. Sew six-inch long ribbons to a washcloth and carry it in your diaper bag so you always have it available. You can pull it out when you need a diversion during your day out on the town.

✳ AIRPLANE

While lying on your back with your knees shut, rest your baby on your raised legs. Give him a gentle ride back and forth, up and down. You will discover what's most comfortable for your baby. Hold on tight, and away you go!

✳ DANCING

While listening to your favorite music, dance around the room together. Depending on your baby's mood (and your own), you can sway softly, rock 'n' roll, or even tango.

✳ BUBBLES

Blow bubbles close so your baby can focus on them, reach for them, and touch them. Enjoy making funny sounds as you blow and pop the bubbles. Use a deep breath to blow the bubbles

*CHANGING TABLE FUN

You spend a lot of time at the changing table when you're taking care of an infant. Before your baby is on the move, you can make this time a lot of fun. Keep a clean, cloth diaper on hand to play "peekaboo" and to tickle your baby's tummy. And keep a list of your favorite songs taped to the wall so you have one ready to sing.

Rock 'n' Roll with Beach Balls

When your baby is about five months old, he might be ready for these beach ball games. Always play them on a carpeted or cushioned floor—spread a large folded quilt to provide a floor pad. Use a beach ball that is about 24 inches in diameter.

*BEACH ROCK

Place your baby on his tummy on the beach ball. Hold onto his thighs with both hands and gently rock and roll him back and forth, over and over again. Create your own words or songs to go with the motion.

*BEACH DRUMS

Place the beach ball in front of your baby. Hold your baby's hands, and tap the ball together with a few simple words, "Tap, tap, tapping on the beach ball." Put on some music, and tap along with it.

*BEACH BOUNCING

Sit your baby on top of a beach ball, holding her at all times around her waist. Straddle the beach ball between your legs so that it doesn't slip out from under your baby and bounce her lightly up and down, singing as you go.

*WATCH THE BALL

Lay your baby on his back on the floor. Throw a beach ball up in the air and catch it above him, over and over again. Babies like to watch the motion and color as the ball floats in the air.

> Check all physical activities for young babies with your practitioner. They are your best advisors for what your baby is ready to do and the appropriate way to hold your baby.

Laptime Sing Along

Young babies spend a lot of time sitting in your lap or resting in your arms. They love and need the closeness, warmth, and security you provide, and songs and rhymes are the perfect way for you to enjoy this time together. You may find yourself singing songs that were sung to you as a child, and it's wonderful to pass these on to your baby. Here's a collection for you to use, gathered from nursery rhymes, folk songs, and old childhood favorites. As your baby grows, add hand movements (suggested movements appear in parentheses throughout). Remember, you can always make up a tune if you don't know one!

> Babies love repetition and will enjoy the same songs and activities over and over. Chances are, you'll tire of them long before your baby does!

*ITSY-BITSY SPIDER

The itsy-bitsy spider went
    up the water spout (climb
    with fingers)
Down came the rain (rain with fingers)
    and washed the spider out (use hands to
    indicate "washed out")
Out came the sun and dried up all the rain (raise
    hands out like sun rising)
And the itsy-bitsy spider went up the spout again
    (climb with fingers)

*THE NOBLE DUKE OF YORK

The Noble Duke of York (with legs out straight,
    bounce baby)
He had ten thousand men
He marched them up to the top of the hill
    (march legs in, bringing knees up)
And he marched them down again
    (knees down, legs back out)

And when you're up, you're up
    (bring knees up fast)
And when you're down, you're down
    (legs back out)
And when you're only halfway up (bring
    knees up slightly)
You're neither up (knees all the way
    up) nor down (legs back out)

He marched them to the left
    (roll baby to left)
He marched them to the
    right (roll baby to right)
He turned them over and upside
    down (roll back, bringing
baby's feet over head)
Oh what a funny sight! (back to original position)

*ON THE WAY TO BOSTON

On the way to Boston (bounce baby)
On the way to Lynn
Hold on tight or you might fall in!
    (hold baby and open your legs so baby falls in)

TWINKLE TWINKLE LITTLE STAR

Twinkle twinkle little star

How I wonder what you are

Up above the world so high

Like a diamond in the sky

Twinkle twinkle little star

How I wonder what

   you are

TEN LITTLE FINGERS AND TOES

(Wiggle each finger or toe as

   you count.)

One little two little three little toesies,

four little five little six little toesies

Seven little eight little nine little toesies

Ten little toesies in a row.

(Repeat with each toe.)

A RUM SUM SUM

A rum sum sum, a rum sum sum

Ooli, gooli, gooli, gooli, gooli

Rum sum sum

A raffi, a raffi

Ooli, gooli, gooli, gooli, gooli,

Rum sum sum (repeat)

BABY, BABY, WASH YOUR FACE

Baby, baby, wash your face

Baby's bath is fun

Baby, baby, wash your face

Now your face is done

(Continue with other body parts.)

PAT A CAKE

Pat a cake, pat a cake,

Baker's man.

Bake me a cake

As fast as you can.

Roll it, and pat it,

And mark it with a "B."

And put it in the oven,

For Baby and me!

*YOU ARE MY SUNSHINE

You are my sunshine, my only sunshine,
You make me happy when skies are gray!
You'll never know, dear, how much I love you
Please don't take my sunshine away!

*HUSH, LITTLE BABY

Hush, little baby, don't say a word
Mamma's going to buy
    you a mockingbird.
If that mockingbird
    don't sing,
Mamma's going to buy
    you a diamond ring.
And if that diamond ring
    turns brass
Mamma's going to buy
    you a looking glass.
And if that looking glass
    gets broke
Mamma's going to buy you a billy goat.
And if that billy goat won't pull
Mamma's going to buy you a cart and bull.
And if that cart and bull turn over
Mamma's going to buy you a dog named Rover.
And if that dog named Rover won't bark
Mamma's going to buy you a horse and cart.
And if that horse and cart fall down
You'll still be the sweetest baby in town.

*FUNNY BUNNY SONG

You're my funny bunny and I love you,
You're my funny bunny and you're grand.
You're my funny bunny and I love you,
You're the best funny bunny in the land!

You're my funny bunny.
You're my funny bunny.

> Your baby hears everything you say and sing. Your talking and singing during these early months lay a foundation for his or her future use of language.

*JACK AND JILL

Jack and Jill went up the hill
To fetch a pail of water.
Jack fell down,
    and broke his crown
And Jill came tumbling after.

*LITTLE RED WAGON

Bumping up and down in my
    little red wagon
Bumping up and down in my little red wagon
Bumping up and down in my little red wagon
Won't you be my darling?

*I'M A LITTLE BABY

I'm a little baby
Yes, I am!
I'm a little baby
That's who I am!

You're growing!

Little Explorers

Six To Twelve Months

Little Explorers
Six to Twelve Months

With the security and foundation you've provided so far, in these months the world opens up for your baby, and your baby draws you into her world. She's friendly, smiles at you, and pulls your ears and nose as she explores everything within reach.

Now there are new skills to master. She learns to sit. He begins to crawl, sometimes backward before forward, pursuing what he wants with great determination. She pulls herself up on her own two feet and cruises around, holding on for support. Some babies take their first steps in these months, but for others, first steps will come later on. Overall, babies at this age develop better control of their hands and learn to hold their own spoons, bottles, and cups. Some can even feed themselves, using their fingers or a spoon—but keep your sponge handy!

During these months, your baby's babbling increases. When you talk to your baby, she understands much of what you say and begins to talk with you in her own fashion. Your baby may speak her first words, although they are probably recognizable only to you. For other babies, it may be a while until they speak.

From six to twelve months, babies begin to understand more of what is happening around them. Life is more predictable, and routines are now more established. Babies become more aware of when you're not there, and they clearly—and often loudly—communicate their wish for your return. You are, after all, the center of their universe, and they love you very deeply.

At this age, babies have more time, energy, skill, and readiness to play. They become fascinated with cause and effect, and they love to repeat what they've learned to do. They love games in which things disappear and reappear—this is the grand age for peekaboo.

The activities in this chapter will challenge your baby's energy and curiosity to explore the world. They are filled with surprises, movement, and lots to do over and over again. As babies become familiar with each game and song, they anticipate with glee what comes next. Their enthusiasm and eagerness to play is contagious—catch it!

Let's Get Moving

Staying in one place becomes a thing of the past for six- to twelve-month-olds. They can sit, crawl, push, pull, and get ready to stand up in the world. These activities will keep you and your baby on the move.

There's no "right" or "wrong" way to use a beach-ball, a hula hoop, or a scarf. These suggestions can get you started. Let your own ideas and playfulness take it from there.

*PILLOW MOUNTAINS

Put some pillows or cushions on the floor so that your baby can crawl across them. If he is really starting to cruise, you can place them next to a couch and let him climb on the pillows while holding onto the couch, with you there beside him. Change the arrangement of the pillows or play in a new room for variety. Have fun climbing the mountains!

*CHAIR CRUISING

Encourage your standing baby's cruising by lining up kitchen chairs firmly against a wall, creating a solid, stable line for her to follow back and forth again. Place a favorite toy at the end as an added incentive to get moving. Your baby will enjoy going from one end to the other, so welcome her with a big smile and hug when she arrives at her destination.

*HULA HOOPS

Hold a hula hoop perpendicular to the floor so that your baby can crawl through it. Lay it flat on the floor for him to crawl in and out. When your baby sits, raise and lower it over his head. Sit together inside the hoop. Your baby can even chase the hoop with a fast crawl as you roll it along with your hand. Round and around you go!

*BUBBLES, BUBBLES EVERYWHERE

Bubbles will be a delightful part of your life for many years to come, but use them according to the age and activity level of your baby. While your baby sits, blow bubbles and let him bat them with his hand. Sit on the floor a few feet away from your baby, blow bubbles, and encourage him to chase and pop them—but don't be surprised if your baby simply sits in one place and watches them float in the air.

*BEACH BALLS II

Beach balls are easily available, inexpensive, lightweight, and colorful toys. Buy a few extra in summertime to have a fresh one to bring out when the weather keeps you in. Roll a beach ball to your baby and let him try to push it back to you. Hold the ball gently in front of your baby and show him how to bat it out of your hands. He may also enjoy crawling after the ball, following it wherever it rolls.

*RING AROUND A ROSY

This old favorite can begin early in your baby's life. Hold your baby and walk around together in a circle, singing,

> **Ring around a rosy, a pocket**
>
> **full of posies,**
>
> **Ashes, ashes, we all fall down.**

Then fall down together. After a few times, you'll notice your child enthusiastically antici-pates this ending. As your baby begins to stand on her own, walk together in a circle. This song is great fun to sing and act out with friends as your children grow, and can actually make a circle together.

*EMPTY CONTAINERS

Leave an assortment of large clean plastic containers on the floor for your baby to play with, some with tops, some without. She'll crawl to them, pick them up, throw them down, exam-ine the different sizes and shapes and have a great time putting them in her mouth. As she gets older, stacking them or nesting them becomes a new game. Try putting a small toy or ball inside one enclosed container for your baby to shake and eventually open and play with.

*SCARVES

One or two lightweight, inexpensive scarves are good to keep on hand. Slowly wave them in front of your baby who will enjoy watching the color and movement and will feel the light breeze as the scarf goes by. Older babies love to reach for the scarves and feel the fabric.

Your baby grows quickly. An acti-vity that seems inconceivable or inappropriate at six months may be just right three months later, so save the idea for the right moment and try again.

✳SHEET GAME

Have your baby sit or lie on his back. Use a baby sheet or blanket to wave up and down over him while you sing,

> The parachute goes up and down,
>
> up and down, up and down,
>
> The parachute goes up and down,
>
> my fair lady

to the tune of "London Bridge" or another favorite.

✳SHEET GAME II

Place the sheet lightly over your baby and say, "Where's (baby's name)?" Raise the side in front of her and say, "There you are!"

✳SHEET GAME III

You'll need two adults for this next game. On a carpeted floor or soft surface, seat your baby in the middle of the sheet or blanket. Take him for a motorboat ride—each grown-up holds two sides of the sheet, making sure it's taut. Walk together, chanting,

> Motorboat, motorboat, go so slow,
>
> Motorboat, motorboat, go so fast,
>
> Motorboat, motorboat, step on the gas.

Begin very slowly to walk in a circle, then walk a little faster. Increase your speed only to the pleasure level of your child. Some children are happy to sit or move slightly, but others enjoy fast motion.

✳HIDE-AND-SEEK GAMES

Knowing that you'll come back makes a beginning version of hide-and-seek a playtime favorite.

Begin by announcing "I'm going to hide." Move to a close and easily accessible spot, like the side of a chair or around a corner, where your baby can still partially see you. Call out for your baby to come and find you, and give him a big hug when he does. Eventually, your baby will begin to hide from you. You'll be playing this game and its more advanced forms for many years to come.

Variation: While your baby is watching, put one of her toys under a small cover so part of it is still visible. Ask "Where did it go?" Babies love pulling off the cover and finding the missing toy.

Your crawling baby's curiosity and determination draw her to whatever is within reach. Set aside a low shelf or kitchen cupboard for a few of her toys or books. You then have a destination that's okay for her to explore.

Making Music

You've already sung to your baby, so shake, rattle, and roll as you begin to make music together!

*KITCHEN INSTRUMENTS

Give your child an assortment of pots and pans and let her make her own music with wooden spoons. Listen together for different sounds. Make a rattle by placing dried beans or rice in a plastic container and taping it securely closed. Try banging a metal lid on a metal pot.

*SONGS FOR BELLS

A set of child-sized hand or wrist bells are great for making music together. Shaking them is lots of fun. Make sure that the bells are safe for your child to use or wait until he is a bit older. Meanwhile, shake them yourself to add to your music listening.

*THE BELL SONG

(Child's name) has a bell, she rings it very well
   (keep ringing)
High (hold bell high, and ring), low (hold bell
   low, and ring)
High low, (child's name) rings her bell.

*ARE YOU SLEEPING?

Are you sleeping, are you sleeping,
   brother John, brother John?
Morning bells are ringing, morning
   bells are ringing
Ding ding dong, ding ding dong.

Sing Along

Develop a repertoire of songs that you can enjoy together with your baby. A song is always with you—to play or comfort, as needed. Here are some of our favorites. Add favorites of your own and trade songs with friends. You'll find them on tapes and compact discs, sung by many different children's entertainers.

Hold your baby in your lap and help him move his arms and legs. As he learns to sit, seat him across from you so he can watch and imitate your movements.

*IF YOU'RE HAPPY AND YOU KNOW IT

If you're happy and you know it clap your hands
   (clap twice)
If you're happy and you know it clap your hands
   (clap twice)
If you're happy and you know it and you
   really want to show it,

If you're happy and you know it clap your
    hands (clap twice).

If you're happy and you know it,
    shout hurray . . . (etc.)
If you're happy and you know it,
    stamp your feet . . . (etc.)
If you're happy and you know it,
    nod your head . . . (etc.)
If you're happy and you know it,
    touch your nose . . . (etc.)

*BRINGING HOME A BABY BUMBLEBEE

I'm bringing home a baby bumblebee
Won't my mommy be so proud of me?
I'm bringing home a baby bumblebee
Buzz, buzz, buzz, buzz, buzz.

I'm bringing home a baby crocodile
Won't my mommy wear a great big smile?
I'm bringing home a baby crocodile
Chomp, chomp, chomp, chomp, chomp.

I'm bringing home a baby dinosaur
Won't my mommy fall right through the floor?
I'm bringing home a baby dinosaur
Clomp, clomp, clomp, clomp, clomp.

I'm bringing home a baby kitty cat
Won't my mommy be so proud of that?

I'm bringing home a baby kitty cat
Meow, meow, meow, meow, meow.

*SIX LITTLE DUCKS

Six little ducks that I once knew (hold up
    six fingers)
Fat ones (spread hands), skinny ones (hands
    close together), fair ones too
But the one little duck with the feather on his
    back (wiggle fingers on back)
He led the others with his quack, quack, quack
    (quack with hands)
Quack, quack, quack, quack, quack, quack
He led the others with his quack, quack, quack.

Home from the river they would come (waddle
    with body)
Wibble wobble wibble wobble ho hum hum
But the one little duck with the feather on his back
    (wiggle fingers on back)
He led the others with his quack, quack, quack
    (quack with hands)
Quack, quack, quack, quack, quack, quack
He led the others with his quack, quack, quack.

*BAA, BAA, BLACK SHEEP

Baa, baa, black sheep,
Have you any wool?
Yes, sir, yes, sir,

Three bags full;
One for the master,
And one for the dame,
And one for the little girl
Who lives down the lane.

Baa, baa, black sheep
Have you any wool?
Yes, sir, yes, sir,
Three bags full.

SITTING IN MY HIGH CHAIR

Sitting in my high chair, big chair,
my chair (bounce)
Sitting in my high chair, banging
my spoon! (bang with hand)
Sitting in my high chair, big
chair, my chair
Sitting in my high chair,
feed me soon!

Bring out the carrots, bring
out the peas!
Somebody feed this
baby please!

Sitting in my high chair, big chair, my chair
Sitting in my high chair, banging my spoon!
Sitting in my high chair, big chair, my chair
Sitting in my high chair, feed me soon!

HICKORY DICKORY DOCK

Hickory dickory dock
The mouse ran up the clock
The clock struck one
Down he did run
Hickory dickory dock

ROW, ROW, ROW YOUR BOAT

Row, row, row your boat
Gently down the stream.
Merrily, merrily, merrily, merrily
Life is but a dream.

IT'S RAINING, IT'S POURING

It's raining, it's pouring.
The old man is snoring.
He went to bed and he bumped his head.
He couldn't get up in the morning.
Rain, rain, go away
Come again some other day.

All babies are unique, and enjoy playing in different ways. Follow your baby's lead. Together you'll discover which activities appeal to you.

49

*HEAD, SHOULDERS, KNEES, AND TOES

· Head (touch head) shoulders (touch shoulders)
     knees (touch knees) and toes (touch toes)
Head shoulders knees and toes, knees and toes
Eyes (touch eyes) and ears (touch ears), a mouth
     (touch mouth) and a nose (touch nose)
Head shoulders knees and toes, knees and toes

*DAISY, DAISY

Daisy, Daisy, give me your
     answer true
I'm half crazy over the
     likes of you.
It won't be a stylish
     marriage—
I can't afford a carriage—
But you'll look sweet
     upon the seat
Of a bicycle built for two!

*LONDON BRIDGE

London Bridge is falling down, falling down,
     falling down
London Bridge is falling down
My fair lady.

Take the keys and lock them up, lock them up,
     lock them up
Take the keys and lock them up
My fair lady.

*OH MR. SUN

Oh Mr. Sun, Sun, Mr. Golden Sun
Won't you please shine down on me?
Oh Mr. Sun, Sun, Mr. Golden Sun
Hiding behind a tree.
These little children are asking you
To please come out so we can play with you
Oh Mr. Sun, Sun, Mr. Golden Sun
Won't you please shine down on me?

Older babies enjoy activities that have stopping and starting as part of the fun. They enjoy doing things over and over again, as they begin to anticipate what comes next.

*OPEN SHUT THEM

Open (fists open) shut them
     (fists closed), open
          shut them
Give a little clap, clap, clap
     (clap three times)
Open shut them, open
     shut them
Put them in your lap, lap, lap
     (tap your lap three times)

Creep them, crawl them (use fingertips),
     creep them, crawl them
Right up to your chin, chin, chin (tap chin
     three times)
Open wide your little mouth (open your mouth)
But do not let them in (hide hands behind back)

Here, There, and Everywhere

One-Year-Olds

shopping

Jim's house

car ride

Here, There, and Everywhere
One-Year-Olds

One-year-olds are in love with the world. They greet each day ready to play, laugh, sing, and run, and are eager to be part of the action. On the flip side, as they struggle to explore and move out into the world, toddlers are easily frustrated and upset, and are challenging to live with from moment to moment. Keeping up with a toddler will surely keep you busy and tired, but you'll be laughing through it all.

This year is a year of tremendous change. On their first birthday, some babies crawl, some cruise around, holding onto whatever is nearby for stability, and some walk on their own.

By the time of their second birthday, babies become fully mobile—they walk, climb, and run, moving with greater agility, coordination, and speed. As the year progresses, they gain more control of their bodies. They may climb to the top of the slide, grip a paintbrush, or zoom around on a riding toy.

Toddlers know and understand more than they are able to say. They point to what they are not yet able to name, while you try to figure out what they want. Gradually, language becomes more important and useful to them. Their vocabulary grows, and they delight in their new ability to say what's on their minds. During this year, first words grow into first sentences.

One-year-olds enjoy being with other toddlers, even though they may not play together. And they like being part of everyday family life. They have strong preferences, know what they want, and often make their desires known with great determination. There are times when they seem able to play endlessly—with great energy and focus. And then there are times when they are tired and worn out, ready to climb into your lap and be the babies they still are.

The activities in this chapter will keep you and your toddler busy using stickers, water, paint, glue, and play dough. You'll tap your fingers and march in parades. So push up your sleeves and let the good times roll!

Busy Fingers, Busy Feet

One-year-olds enjoy experiencing the world through their bodies. They are developing a new expertise and freedom in mobility—

A year is a long time in a toddler's life. Pick and choose from these suggestions according to your toddlers interests as well as what he can manage.

walking, running, climbing, jumping. This is an exhilarating time for them.

*A TRIP TO THE ZOO

Children are fascinated by animals, and love to watch how they move, eat, and climb, and to listen to the different sounds animals make. As children approach two years of age, they enjoy imitating their favorite animals—and you can make a game of it.

Take a make-believe trip to the zoo (or farm or pet store). "Let's be elephants and swing our trunks!" "Let's hop like bunnies!" Ducks waddle, turkeys strut, seals flap their flippers, and monkeys swing, scratch, and climb. Have fun roaring like lions together!

quack arf arf roar grrrrr

*BLANKET RIDES

Sit your child in the middle of a blanket, sheet, or towel on the floor. Give your child a ride by gently pulling her around. She will experience a new way to move through space and to see what's around her. Off you go!

*BLANKET PRETEND

Blankets are also great for pretending. Have a picnic or take a car ride with your child, and let your imaginations take hold. Get off and on, and go in and out of your pretend car, house, or boat. Old bathroom throw rugs are great for these activities.

*PARADES

Parades are often a big hit with young toddlers. Put on whatever music you and your baby enjoy most—rock, classical music, and children's songs will work as well as traditional marching band music. Children get to know the music, and their energy inspires them to move.

Take turns being the leader—move in and out of different rooms, and reverse directions. Add clapping, stamping, wiggling, and high-stepping. With a portable tape recorder, you can even bring your parade outdoors. Add bells and drums to accompany the music. Strike up the band as you march along!

*THE TAPPING GAME

Children love chanting games that are short, repetitive, and that bring a surprise at the end. When you're sitting at a table, start tapping and sing,

Tap, tap, tapping on the table,

Tap, tap, tapping on the table,

Tap, tap, tapping on the table,

Till it's time to stop! (raise your

arms up)

Watch how quickly your child catches on and stops tapping, hands up in the air. Try different variations: tapping softly, then louder; slowly, then faster. Eventually, your toddler will become the leader, so get those fingers tapping.

*PUPPETS

Some children begin to enjoy puppets at this age. A puppet can be store-bought or homemade, and a stuffed animal can even be used as a puppet. At this early age, use a puppet when you sing, dance, and play together. This can be an early form of "make-believe" and pretend play. Welcome these new puppet friends to your playtimes.

*THROUGH THE SLOT

Here's a homemade game that keeps your toddler's fingers, eyes, and ears busy all at once. You'll need an empty coffee can with a plastic lid and a collection of large, plastic poker chips (milk bottle caps work well, too). Place heavy tape around the top edge of the can to cover any sharp edges that may remain. Cut a slit in the plastic lid large enough for your chips to fall through. Put on the lid and show your toddler how to push the chips through. She'll enjoy the sound of the chips hitting the can and each other. Stop and shake it. When it's full, empty your can, and start again.

Play Dough

Your child will enjoy using play dough for many years. It is readily avaiable— store-bought or homemade. Either version is easy to use, inexpensive, versatile, and engaging for young children. Young toddlers enjoy feeling the texture of play dough. They love to squeeze, push, pound, roll, and flatten it. And you might enjoy it as well.

Some toddlers dislike getting their hands dirty. Others revel in it. Be sensitive to your child's preference when considering paints, glue, play dough, and other messy materials.

You can make play dough easily at home. Two different recipes are included below. As your toddler gets older, making play dough with you becomes part of the fun. It keeps for many weeks when it is stored in a sealed plastic container. Keep some on hand so you have it ready when you are.

*COOKED PLAY DOUGH

1 cup flour

1 tablespoon oil

1 cup water

½ cup salt

2 teaspoons cream of tartar

Food coloring

1. Mix dry ingredients together in a sauce pan.

2. Add wet ingredients and mix together.

3. Cook over a low to medium flame.

4. Stir constantly to prevent scorching, until the mixture forms into a ball. (No more than five minutes.)

5. Knead until smooth.

6. Store in a sealed plastic container or refrigerate.

(You can also make this recipe without the food coloring. You can then add food coloring as you knead, and observe the process of the white dough changing color together. As your children get older, make larger batches to have on hand.)

*UNCOOKED PLAY DOUGH

This is a great recipe to make with your child as he gets older. Although it doesn't keep as long, or dry as well as the cooked play dough, you can make it quickly, and your child can be part of the process.

2 cups flour

1 cup salt

1 cup water

Food coloring

1. Mix together flour and salt.

2. Add water with food coloring dissolved in it.

3. Knead it together. It may take a few minutes for the dough to form.

You can use play dough on any washable surface—a countertop or tabletop works well, as does a plastic tablecloth spread out on the floor.

For young toddlers, a chunk of dough the size of a tennis ball is good to start with. Fingers are the best molding tool for your toddler to use. Later, add miniature rolling pins, plastic cookie cutters, or a small, lightweight toy hammer. A garlic press is good, too. When your child is older, you can move on to more elaborate activities.

To clean up play dough, get rid of any dry, crusty pieces from your supply before you put the dough away. Use a scraper or textured nylon cleaning pad to scrape off your work surface. If you reserve a plastic tablecloth for play dough, it's not necessary to do a total clean-up. Simply throw away the dry bits and fold up the cloth for next time. Be sure to clean tools completely so that dry pieces of dough do not interfere with your next use. And check the bottom of your shoes before you walk through the house!

Art Starts

At about thirteen months old, your child may be ready to explore some simple art materials. For toddlers, it's the experience of using different materials that's satisfying—a finished product is not so important at this age.

*STICKERS

Children love stickers, but it takes practice for them to be able to pull a sticker off its sheet and place it on a piece of paper. Start by peeling the sticker off partially, to make it easier for your child to grasp and pull it off. Take her hand and show her how to "tap-tap" the sticker onto the paper. If you or someone you know works in an office, ask them to bring home the scrap materials from labels and file

stickers. These are great for children to use, along with stickers that have pictures and designs. Look for and buy reusable sticker books—you can remove the stickers to use over and over again.

*STICKER WALLHANGINGS

Decorate a paper plate with stickers. Punch a hole at the top of the plate, put a piece of yarn through it, and hang it on your wall or bulletin board. Watch your collection of sticker art grow!

> It's a great temptation to direct your child's art project: "Stay inside the lines...add more stickers...why not use blue?" Try to resist this impulse and let your child be the artist.

*STICKER CROWNS

For your child's birthday, cut out a crown from his favorite color construction paper. Have him decorate it with stickers. Staple the crown so that it fits around your child's head. Cover the staple with a piece of scotch tape on the inside of the crown so that it doesn't catch on your child's hair. Let your child be king for a day!

*STICKER VASES

Take an empty plastic soda bottle and have your child decorate it with stickers. Fill your vase with real or paper flowers, and place it where the entire family can enjoy it.

*STICKER AND CRAYON MURALS

Young children often find it difficult to confine themselves to a small piece of paper, so a roll of brown paper, white shelf paper, or the back of used wrapping paper are good large art surfaces to keep on hand. Lay out a large piece and a few thick, easy-to-handle crayons. After your child is finished drawing, he can add stickers.

*STICKER HANDS AND FEET

On a big piece of paper, trace your child's hands and feet. Have her color them and decorate them with stickers. It doesn't matter if the decorations stay inside the lines or out. Make new hands and feet from time to time, and look together at how she has grown!

*DRAWING BOOKS

Give your child a small memo book from the stationery store. He'll be proud that it belongs to him, and it's easy to travel with. Don't forget the crayons, so that wherever you go, he'll always have something to do.

*PAINTING WITH WATER

Dip a paintbrush in water so that your child can "paint" on a chalkboard. Watch the chalkboard change color as it gets wet and then dries. Children love to repeat this again and again. A sponge also works well for this activity. Go paint a water masterpiece!

*OUTDOOR WATER PAINTING

A paintbrush and a small plastic bucket are great additions to your collection of outdoor playground or backyard toys. Fill up the bucket with water, and your toddler can paint the fence, the trees, or your driveway.

*PAINTING WITH COLORED WATER

Add a few drops of food coloring to an inch of water, and your child can paint on paper. Food coloring is easy and quick to use. It may

> Anything can be a smock. If your child resists wearing a smock, offer her one of your old T-shirts or button-down shirts instead. Call it her painting shirt.

temporarily color the skin, but it comes off with soap and water.

*TISSUE PAPER AND WATER

Cut shapes from colored tissue paper. Have your child place them on a piece of paper and then "paint" them with water. After they're dry, remove the tissue paper so you're left with a colorful "watercolor" painting. Your art collection is growing!

*WATERCOLORS

Older toddlers may be ready to enjoy using watercolors. Look for simple sets that have only a few large cakes of color—these are easy for beginners to use. Also, try to use a thick-handled brush that fits a toddler's grip.

Teaching your child how to use watercolors is a step-by-step process. Help her dip the brush lightly in water to keep it from getting too soggy. Touch the brush to a sponge or paper towel to absorb the excess water. Dab the brush into the paint, and make your picture! "Dip, dip, wipe, wipe, paint, paint" is a handy saying for this process. Start with one color and gradually add more.

*FINGERPAINTS

Older toddlers can use non-toxic fingerpaints in an aluminum pan or on a large piece of paper. Some children will use only the tip of one finger to make a line, while others will use both hands exhuberantly to spread the paint over the entire paper. Don't forget to keep water handy for cleaning up. Grab your camera and capture the messy moment—fingers, face, and picture.

> Keep an assortment of small, inexpensive housepainting brushes on hand to use for various activities.

*TIRE TRACKS

Have your child roll one of his small toy cars through water-based tempera paint, then roll it over a piece of paper. Do this in different directions for an interesting design of colored tire tracks. A miniature paint roller from the hardware store also works well. When you're done, roll your cars into the car wash—your sink, a plastic tub, or a hose outside. Cleaning up is as much fun as painting!

* TWIN PRINTS

Fold a large piece of paper in half. Paint on one side only, fold the paper over with your child, and press down firmly together. When you unfold the paper, you'll have a mirror image! Watch your child's face when he sees the results!

*CARDBOARD ROLLS

Even a young toddler can make a home decoration. Use the empty rolls from paper towels or toilet paper, and paint and decorate them. Then cut them into different size pieces. String the pieces together with heavy yarn to make a decoration that hangs on the wall or on a doorknob. These hangings also make great mobiles.

*GLUE PICTURES

Dripping glue is fun for children to play with as they watch the lines cross, and emerge into a design. Use colored glue and squeeze the bottle directly on paper. Using different colors of paper adds variety for both of you. Try paper plates or the inside of a box top. You'll soon have an entire gallery of glue pictures.

It may take a while for young children to grasp the concept of gluing. Show them how glue works by putting a dab of glue on a piece of paper, and tapping a shape onto it. "See how it stays on?" Then tap a shape onto the paper without glue. "See how it falls off?"

*CONTACT PAPER PLACEMATS

Take a piece of clear contact paper and place it on the table, sticky side up. Tape the corners down so it doesn't wiggle. Have your child make a collage, adding scraps of greeting cards, wrapping paper, newspaper, aluminum foil, tissue paper, yarn— anything you have in the house. Use different textures, like felt and lace. When your child is finished, cover it with another piece of clear

contact paper. Make this your child's very own placemat at mealtimes. She can even make one for each member of the family! Use the technique with a construction paper backing to make colorful collages to hang on your walls.

Hands in the Water

Water is a natural part of your toddler's daily experience. They drink it, bathe in it, see rain and puddles. And some children also enjoy playing with it.

A plastic tablecloth on the floor of the kitchen or bathroom and a plastic basin filled with a few inches of water can provide a wonderful time for you and your toddler together. Always stay with your child when using water. Small sponges, squeeze bottles, and measuring cups with spouts are all great water toys.

*BATHING A DOLL

Toddlers know what a bath is and often enjoy giving the bath. Give your child a small, waterproof doll and a sponge, so that he can play "bathtime." A dry washcloth can be the towel to dry the "baby" with after the bath. Your child might enjoy repeating the same bathtime games and songs that you do with him, and you can give the doll a special bubble bath by adding a small amount of non-toxic blowing bubbles to the water. Your child will have the cleanest collection of dolls in town!

*WASHING TOYS

Some toys are suitable for washing and can be added to a basin of water for playtime—and for real, honest-to-goodness cleaning. Plastic or rubber trucks, boats, and animals are great additions to water play.

Hands in the Sand

One-year-olds love to fill, pour, and empty containers. Sand is ideal for these activities because it feels great, and toddlers can scoop it up and pour it out endlessly. Indoors or out, you can create your own portable temporary "sandbox" so that sand play is always a possibility.

Sand and water are engaging for toddlers—they bring their own individual style of play to these materials. Some toss sand and splash water with gusto, while others will explore quietly in great detail. As your toddler grows, his style may change. Be open to new possibilities.

*SAND PLAY

Take an old shower curtain or tarp and lay it on the floor or the ground. Place a large plastic basin with low sides in the middle of the tarp, and fill it with two inches of sand (inexpensive bags of sanitized sand are sold at toy and home stores). Seat your child outside the basin and give her an assortment of kitchen utensils—funnels, small plastic bowls, thoroughly cleansed measuring cups from detergent bottles—to use.

Play along with your toddler to encourage her interest in exploring the sand. Pour sand through a funnel so she can try to catch it. Let her bury her hand or a small toy, and then uncover it. When it's time to clean up, simply fold the shower curtain and funnel the excess sand back into a bag or container. Store all the sand toys in the basin, ready for the next time.

Plastic pans made for holding kitty litter are just the right size, shape, and depth for sand and water play.

Some children will try to eat sand, so cornmeal is a good sand substitute. However, because spoons are associated with eating, be sure to eliminate them as utensils in sand or cornmeal play until your child is older.

Sing Along

By now, you have your own favorite songs, nursery rhymes, and finger plays that you enjoy together. Here are some new songs to try indoors and out.

*RING AROUND A ROSY

Ring around a rosy
A pocket full of posies
Ashes, ashes, we all fall down!

The cows are in the meadow
They're huddled all together
There's thunder and lightning
(pound on the floor)
And we all jump up!

*I'M RIDING IN MY CAR

I'm riding in my car
I'm riding in my car
I'm riding in my car
across the avenue.
Oh driver, won't you stop

Oh driver, won't you stop
Oh driver, won't you stop
until the light turns green?

*HERE COMES THE CHOO CHOO TRAIN

Here comes our choo choo train
Coming down the track
First it's going forward
Then it's going back
Hear the bells ringing, ding a ling,
ding a ling
Hear the whistle blowing, woo woo
What a lot of noise it makes
Everywhere it goes!

*HERE WE GO LOOPDI LOO

Here we go loopdi loo
Here we go loopdi lei
Here we go loopdi loo
All on a Saturday night.
I put my right hand in
I take my right hand out
I give my right hand
a shake, shake, shake
And turn myself around
(repeat, with different body parts)

*ONE LITTLE, TWO LITTLE BUBBLES

One little, two little, three little bubbles
Four little, five little, six little bubbles
Seven little, eight little, nine little bubbles
Ten little bubbles in the air.

Let's pop, pop, pop those bubbles
Pop, pop, pop those bubbles
Pop, pop, pop those bubbles
Pop them in the air.

*THREE LITTLE MONKEYS

Three little monkeys jumping on the bed
One fell off and bumped his head!
Mamma called the doctor, and the doctor said,
"No more monkeys jumping on the bed!"

Two little monkeys . . . (etc.)
One little monkey . . . (etc.)

*SWING SONG

Way high
Up in the sky
(Child's name) is going to fly
(Repeat)

*SKY SONG

The moon is in the sky,
The leaves are on the trees.
The birds are in the air,
They're flying everywhere.

*MARY HAD
A LITTLE LAMB

Mary had a little lamb,
    Its fleece was white as snow,
And everywhere that Mary went
    The lamb was sure to go;
He followed her to school one day—
    That was against the rule,
It made the children laugh and play
    To see a lamb at school.

A lot taller!

Start!

glue

straws

styrofoam balls

paintbrush

crayon

shoe box

buttons

construction paper

paper dolls

Ready, Set, Go!

duck

sailboat

snowman

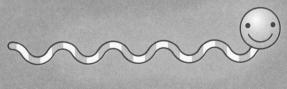

worm

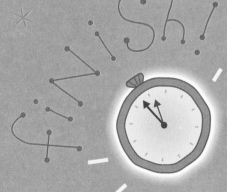

Finish!

Ready, Set, Go!
Two-Year-Olds

Two-year-olds are terrific. Playful, affectionate, humorous, curious, and very imaginative, they are great observers and are full of questions. They actively strive to make sense of their world, although their conclusions are not always accurate. They enjoy helping in their own unique fashion—and imitating the adults around them.

Two-year-olds become aware that they are growing up. During this year, many toddlers move into a bed, and stop wearing diapers. They learn to play more independently, attempting to try new things on their own. "I can do it myself," they say over and over again. They enjoy playing with other children and anticipate the good time they'll have when a friend comes to visit.

On the other hand, two-year-olds can also be trying, stubborn, strong-willed, and extremely uncooperative. They are determined to do things their own way. Reason and logic have no place in a two-year-old's thinking. So some moments can be difficult and exhausting.

Two-year-olds are busy. Their days are full of physical activity morning, noon, and night, generally refreshed by a nap at some point during the day. Gradually, they acquire impressive new skills, and enjoy sorting, sequencing, and learning shapes and colors.

Pretend and make-believe are major parts of their everyday play. They dress up as mommy or daddy, play house or store, and begin to understand and participate in the world more fully.

These new interests and skills open new possibilities for what you can do together. In this chapter, you'll dance with scarves, make fabulous presents, design your own wrapping paper, and cook up a storm! But you might want to begin with a warm-up stretch in the morning to get going.

Moving On and Make-Believe

Two-year-olds enjoy games and activities that challenge their boundless physical energy. Take a deep breath and off you go together!

⋇ WARM UP STRETCH

Have your child sit across from you, legs straight out. Have him follow along with you. Say "hello" (point your hands and feet out), "goodbye" (flex your hands and feet), "yes" (nod your head a couple of times), "no" (shake your head from side to side), "maybe so" (stretch your arms to the side), and "I don't know" (shrug your shoulders). Repeat several times, and a rhythm develops. This stretch is easy to do throughout the day, wherever you might be.

⋇ PEEKABOO STRETCH

Here's another good stretching exercise. Have your child sit across from you, cross-legged and rounded over, with her head down into her chest. Say "Peekaboo!" and slowly straighten out, stretching on the way up. Repeat this several times. Add a "Peekaboo!" to the left and to the right. Whisper "Peekaboo!" then shout it.

⋇ HULA HOOP HOPSCOTCH

Set up hula hoops on the floor to look like a hop-scotch board or any other design you like. Two-year-olds are not yet able to hop on one foot, but they have a great time jumping from one hoop to the next on both feet.

As they get older, show them how to land with one foot in hoops that are touching each other. They can then jump with both feet into the next hoop.

⋇ HULA HOOP JOURNEYS

Hula hoops are very versatile, and together your imaginations can take you on many magical journeys with them. While holding a hula hoop in his hands, your child can make believe that he is driving a car, a bus, or an airplane. Have your child hold onto the hoop while you gently pull him along to your destination. It's fun to stop at a red light, make a right turn, or go over the mountain, and upon arrival, sit down together inside the hoop as you explore your new place. So off you go to see the world!

> Some two-year-olds are more physically active than others. Some will stay with an activity for quite a while, but others will need to move on to something new. Be patient and attentive to your child's needs.

> Your enthusiasm is contagious. If you enjoy an activity, your child is more likely to give it a try.

*OBSTACLE COURSE

You can set up a simple obstacle course at home using pillows, cushions, cardboard boxes, children's step stools, sturdy chairs, hula hoops, and masking tape. The path can include climbing over, under, through, in, out, and around things. Use masking tape to make starting and finishing lines, and even arrows to follow.

Children love variation, so you can arrange your obstacle course differently each time—but don't be surprised if your child wants to repeat an especially good one. Let them help you set up and direct the course. You might be surprised by their ingenuity!

*MORNING JOG

Begin your day together by taking a morning jog around the house together. Talk about what you see along the way as you run "laps." Count how many laps you run. Running with your toddler will keep you both in shape.

*MARIONETTE STRETCH

Sit on the floor, legs spread out. Use your hands to pretend you're pulling the strings of a marionette to raise or move the different parts of your body. You and your child can do this with your own bodies, and then take turns pulling strings on each other. Say "Let's pull up your foot," as you pull on an imaginary string. Your child slowly lifts her foot. Then move on to the next foot, the arms, and the head. You might also enjoy looking at a real marionette together to see how it works.

*SPIDER STRETCHES

Lie on your back. Raise your arms and legs up in the air. Use your arms and legs, hands and feet, as if you are climbing into the air like a many-legged spider. Don't forget to wiggle your fingers and toes to spin your "web!"

*BICYCLES

Two-year-olds have seen older children pedal their bicycles, and eventually they will be able to do it themselves. Meanwhile, bicycle in the air together. Lie on your back, with your feet up in the air. Pedal with your legs as though you're riding a bicycle. Chat about where you are going. Slow down. Go faster. Make a short stop. Don't forget to signal!

*DONKEY KICKS AND KANGAROO HOPS

Have your child get down on all fours. Pretend you're both donkeys and kick back one foot at a time. Bray like a donkey. Be wiggly worms or snakes sliding on the floor, birds flying through the air, or kangaroos hopping across the outback.

*SCARF GAME

Lightweight scarves make great, inexpensive props. Pick up half a dozen differently colored scarves at the five and dime, and let your child's imagination loose. Give him time to explore the texture and feel its airiness. Put on music and dance around, wearing your scarves.

*SCARF TOSS

Put on some music and play catch, tossing scarves in the air, and watch them float and fly into your hands.

> Scarves are easy to use outdoors. Try these activities outside in a large open space.

*SCARF JUMP ROPE

Tie several scarves end to end, or to a door-knob, and turn them jump-rope style.

*MONSTER DANCE

Let your child place a scarf over her head or hold it in front of her face, pretending she's a ghost or a monster. She can "monster walk" around, trying to catch you.

*BODY CATCH

Have your child throw a scarf in the air. Name the part of the body he should use to catch it. Ask him to catch it, "On your head!" "On your finger!" "On your foot!" Switch roles as your child names the body parts for you.

*TORO! TORO!

Hold a scarf in front of you, sideways, like a bullfighter. Let your child run into it and toss the scarf over her.

*MAGIC CARPET

Use a large scarf as a magic carpet. Sit on it together and pretend you're on a journey. Talk about where you're flying and get off to explore. Hop back on and off you go to a new destination. Be sure to be home by bedtime!

*BALANCE BEAMS

Line up narrow scarves or long pieces of yarn to make a beginning "balance beam." Your child can walk along it, one foot in front of the other. Try variations—walk with one foot on each side of the line, walk backward, or jump.

✳ PAINT THE SKY

Use a scarf to paint the sky. Talk about the different colors you're using. Reach high to touch the clouds, the moon, and the stars.

✳ TURN AROUND

Have your child toss a scarf into the air, then turn around quickly and try to catch it before it touches the ground.

> Two-year-olds are just learning to follow directions. Be patient if they reinvent the game in their own unique way.

✳ COSTUMES

Scarves make great toddler-size costumes. Two or three will do for an entire toddler! Use one for a sash, one for a hat, and one for a cape.

✳ TAPE SHAPES

Use thick, colored tape to make large shapes on the floor or to make shapes with chalk outside on the sidewalk or driveway. Call out different movements—"March to the triangle," "Tiptoe to the circle," "Run to the square." Walk backward. Take tiny steps. Take giant steps. Jump from one shape to another. Then, let your child do the calling. This game will keep you on your toes!

✳ TOSSED SALAD

You can use construction paper to make colorful vegetables and tape them to the floor instead of shapes. Large magazine pictures glued to paper also work. Then, call out different movements again—"Jump to the carrot," "Walk backward to the tomato," "Hop to the cucumber." You'll work up a great appetite, tossing your salad.

✳ THE LIMBO

Decorate an empty wrapping paper roll with crayons, markers, or stickers. Hold one end and place the other against a wall, or have another person hold it. Tell your child to walk or crawl under it as you lower the limbo stick a little bit with each turn. Add some lively music. This is a great activity to do with several children together.

✳ CHOO CHOO

Place your hands on your child's waist and have her take you on a choo choo train ride around the house. Your train can make stops along the way, and other passengers can hop on board the train as you stop at the station to pick them up, shouting "All Aboard!" Add a train song or two as you go down the track. Don't get off until the end of the line!

PIZZA SLICES

Cut out slices of pizza from construction paper and place them on the floor, in a line, or in a circle. Jump over the slices. Run around them, but don't land in the sticky cheese!

MIME

Two-year-olds love to act out the words of songs and rhymes. Be the mouse who runs up the clock in "Hickory Dickory Dock." Be Humpty Dumpty falling off the wall, or Little Bo Peep searching for her sheep. Listen for songs to act out as you sing them. For instance, (to the tune of "Here We Go Round the Mulberry Bush"),

This is the way we wash our face . . .

This is the way we comb our hair . . .

This is the way we brush our teeth . . .

This is the way we tie our shoes . . .

You can also mime everyday experiences. "Let's cook breakfast together!" Open the pretend cabinet door and take out the invisible box of cereal. Reach for a bowl. Grab a spoon. Open the pretend refrigerator to get the milk. Pour everything into the bowl and eat it all up!

Try, "Let's get dressed." "Let's get ready for bed." "Let's go to the supermarket." You'll have a wonderful time miming everything together.

FREEZE DANCE

Put on some music and dance to it together, then stop the music suddenly while you freeze in place. Wiggle, jump, fly, or crawl to the music—then freeze. Each time, vary how long you wait before stopping. Two-year-olds love surprises.

BUBBLES II

By now, your child is very familiar with bubbles. As you blow the bubbles, play games by chasing, popping, counting, or catching them. As your child learns to blow bubbles himself, ask him to blow high or low, in front of or behind his friend, above or below your finger.

CAR WASH

Two-year-olds often have a favorite riding toy. On a warm, sunny afternoon, choose a good spot for a car wash—a grassy lawn or a sidewalk will do. Give your child a large sponge and a bucket filled halfway with water and non-toxic bubbles, and let

Two-year-olds are not fully in control of their bodies. A good try and a good time are what's really important. As you try movement activities throughout the year, you will notice significant changes in your child's agility and coordination.

her wash away! Use a large, old bath towel for drying. Your child will feel proud as she pulls away in her shiny vehicle!

CARPET SQUARES

Carpet squares make great special spaces for games. Children can jump from one to the next one. Use them as magic carpets, buses, or spaceships. Add them to your obstacle courses. And as your children get older, play "Musical Carpet Squares," a more manageable variation on musical chairs.

Art Smarts

Shape, color, texture, paint, glue, collage— two-year-olds are ready to explore it all. And they are great artists!

TREASURE BOXES

Empty egg cartons are perfect for storing your child's treasures. After painting or coloring a carton, decorate it with stickers, or glue on shapes made from construction paper, wrapping paper, or magazine pictures. Treasure boxes make great presents for special people.

> Art is a messy business. Dress yourself and your child accordingly, and don't worry about getting dirty—you will!

PLAY DOUGH PLAY FOOD

Children enjoy making food items out of play dough. Pound it, roll it, shape it to make pizza, pancakes, or spaghetti, and have a pretend meal. Add toy dishes or paper plates to enhance the fun at your party or picnic. (For play dough recipes and suggestions, see page 57.)

PLAY DOUGH SCULPTURES

With a few popsicle sticks, your child can make imaginative sculptures out of play dough. Add beads and buttons to make complex sculptures, and let them air dry. Then you can paint her sculpture together. You can even shellac the piece if you want to save it.

PLAY DOUGH HANDS AND FEET

Together, on a sheet of paper, make a large flat play dough pancake, at least one inch thick. Make a handprint or footprint, then let it dry and paint it. These are wonderful to save or to give as gifts.

BOX SCULPTURES

Help your child to make a large sculpture by gluing different size boxes together— food boxes, shoe boxes, or jewelry gift boxes.

> It's not necessary to buy a closetful of art materials. Use your imagination and look at basic materials in new ways.

Decorate them by gluing on whatever you'd like—soft feathers, fabric scraps, or colorful paper provide an interesting contrast of textures.

*PASTA JEWELRY

Beading can be fun for two-year-olds, but most beads are too difficult for small hands to manage. Dry pasta, in a variety of shapes and colors, is a good alternative.

Use a length of yarn on which to string the pasta. Dip the ends of the yarn into a little glue, and let them dry—this will make the ends needle-like, and easier for your child to slip through the pasta hole.

Your two-year-old can make an original set of pasta jewelry—bracelets, necklaces, and belts. Ziti is a good shape to use, but try wagon wheels, dinosaurs, or teddy bear shapes for variety.

Children can paint the pasta first with tempera paint, or adults can combine food coloring with a little water to dye the pasta beforehand. Hold each piece, dip it into the dye, and count to ten. Place the pasta on paper towels to dry.

> Never use glitter with young children. It is unsafe. Glitter consists of tiny metal pieces and can be harmful to your child's eyes.

Food coloring is messy and stains your fingers, but also works successfully for this activity. Prepare your beads the day before you plan to use them. Your child's "pasta originals" will be fun to wear at home and to give as presents.

*SNACKLACES

For an edible alternative, substitute any kind of "O" cereal for the dry pasta. Small pretzels are great fun to work with, and these snacklaces are great to carry around for your child to nibble on!

*MAKE YOUR OWN MOBILE

Cut out a familiar shape—a fish, house, ice-cream cone, boat, or car. Use heavy paper such as cardboard, brown wrapping paper, or even a cut-up gift box. Aim for a size about twelve inches square to have an inviting surface to decorate. Get your child busy with crayons, large stickers, paint, and collage materials. Hang the finished art on a string where everyone can see it, or make a few and string them together as a mobile.

> Art is more enjoyable if you don't have to worry about making a mess. Place a big old plastic tablecloth or several garbage bags under your work surface so you don't have to think twice about ruining a floor or carpet.

*TISSUE PAPER TREES

Cut out a wide piece of brown construction paper to use as a tree trunk. Let your child add leaves— crumple small pieces of colored tissue paper, dip them in glue and stick them on the tree. As the seasons change, make a new tree based on what you see together outside.

Young children sometimes have a tendency to work on one corner of a piece of paper. Gently refocus them and give them a new perspective by saying, "Let's see what happens when we turn the paper a little."

*COTTON SWAB PAINTING

Cotton swabs fit perfectly into a two-year-old's hand. Use them as paintbrushes. Children can dip the swab into the paint and make dots by dabbing the paper all over. Show them how to make broad strokes as well as short lines and dots. No need to wash your brushes— toss them when done!

*CATALOG COLLAGES

Children love to use glue. Save your old catalogs, especially those with toys and children's clothing. Choose favorite pictures together and cut them out for your child. Then he can make a wonderful catalog collage.

*WRAPPING PAPER COLLAGES

Save wrapping paper from birthday presents and holiday gifts. Keep a box of pieces cut into a variety of shapes and sizes, then your child can choose her favorite designs and make a collage by gluing pieces onto paper. Add tissue paper scraps for more color.

*PASTA COLLAGES

Offer your child an assortment of pasta shapes to glue onto a piece of thick cardboard. Vary this activity by using different colored pasta or glue.

*STAMPING WITH CORKS

Save your wine corks—these make wonderful stamps for your child. Grip the cork at one end, holding it upright. Dip it into tempera paint and stamp the painted end on paper. Wine cork stamps on newspaper or tissue paper make great homemade wrapping paper.

Give your artist a new perspective by varying the size and shape of his paper. Move beyond the standard rectangle. Add circles, long panels, or non-symmetrical shapes.

*COOKIE CUTTER PRINTS

Plastic cookie cutters (avoid metal ones), especially ones with grippable handles, make other handy printing tools. Look for familiar shapes—teddy bears, hearts, circles, squares, and gingerbread people. Start with one color at a time, and then introduce color mixing.

> Paper plates are also fun to work on. Avoid styrofoam or plastic coated plates which repel glue and paint.

*SPONGE PAINTING

Cut sponges into an assortment of different shapes and sizes. Dip the sponge into thick tempera paint and stamp it on paper. The sponge

> Extend your child's interest and involvement by adding small amounts of one material at a time. Toddlers become overwhelmed by too much to choose from.

will absorb a lot of paint. It's fun for your child to paint broad strokes, using his whole arm, to fill a large piece of paper. Keep these sponges for use with paint only.

*STICKERS

At two, your child becomes more proficient with stickers and enjoys using them. Keep a good supply on hand—stickers are a wonderful diversion on long car rides and can be added to other art work.

*WATER PAINTING

Painting with water is still a fun activity, both indoors and out. For a two-year-old, try an assortment of different size brushes. Paint on a chalkboard or a large piece of brown paper which doesn't get soggy. When a playmate visits, use a very large piece of paper and paint a water line down the middle so each child can "paint" on his own side. Water, water, everywhere!

*PAINTING WITH FOOD COLORING

Mix water with a few drops of food coloring as an alternative to watercolors or tempera paints. Children love to use this new kind of "paint" on paper towels. The colors will bleed and blend, and will make interesting patterns and designs. It's fun to watch it happen before your very own eyes. Remember that food coloring stains your fingers until it wears off, and wear smocks, too.

*WATERCOLORS

Two-year-olds love the ritual of using water-colors—dipping the brush in water, wiping off the excess, and touching the brush to the paint. Show them how to use these paints one color at a time so they can really see each color fully in their work. Watercolors work best on plain white paper. Look for simple sets with a few large cakes of paint. For other suggestions about using watercolors, see page 61.

*TISSUE PAPER COLLAGE

Here's a basic technique which you can adapt in many ways—use it to make a collage on paper, to decorate boxes, to make wrapping paper, or to cover a coffee can as a special container.

Tear tissue paper into manageable pieces. Make a mixed solution of water and a small amount of glue. Have your child place a piece of tissue on a sheet of paper, and paint over it with the glue solution, covering it completely. Add more pieces, overlapping their edges, and "paint" each piece into place. Be careful not to oversaturate the work. The finished product will be a beautiful mosaic of color and shape.

*FINGERPAINTS

If your child will try fingerpaints, get ready for some down and dirty fun! If she is reluctant, you try it first, and show her how easily the paint washes off. Set up non-toxic fingerpaints on a roomy surface—a large piece of paper, a formica counter or tabletop, or a large aluminum roasting pan. Begin with a spoonful of one color

and add more as you go along. Some children paint with one fingertip—others with their whole hand. Enjoy your child's own style. For variety, your child can add a second color, turning yellow and blue into green, or red and blue into purple.

Prepare for clean-up before you get started— keep a basin of water, paper towels, and a large, wet sponge available. Then put on your smocks, roll up your sleeves, and have a great time!

Here's a tip for using glue: Pour a small amount into a large jar lid or a small paper plate. Use a cotton swab as a glue brush.

*DRIPPING GLUE

Squeeze a container of glue over paper to make a design. Use colored glue for added interest. Your child can then let the paper dry as a glue picture or add other materials to make a collage. Take out your scrap paper box and have your child choose a few items to embellish the design.

Make your own colored glue by mixing a little paint into a cup of white glue.

*DOT, DOT, DOT

Children love to make dot pictures, and older two-year-olds find "dot making" especially appealing. Use crayons and markers, compare the different sounds they make, and notice the different dots that appear. You may end up creating your own "Dot" song to accompany your work.

＊FEATHER PAINTING

Try painting with feathers for a little variety. Use large quill pen-type feathers with enough space for your child to grip. Tempera paint works well for this activity. See what happens when you tickle the paper with your feather?

＊PAINT PRINTS

Pour paint into an aluminum tray. Have your child dip a potato masher into the paint, then print it on a piece of paper. These prints make unique wrapping paper. Try the same technique with other "printers" that your child can manage—half a potato, a slotted spoon, or a large chunk of carrot.

> Cooking together with your child may bring to life your own childhood memories of being in the kitchen. These are nice memories to share with your children.

＊WATERCOLOR AND CRAYONS

Draw a picture or a design with crayons on plain white paper. Use watercolors to paint over it, filling in the empty spaces on the paper. Watch how the paint changes the crayon picture.

Kids in the Kitchen

Two-year-olds can be great chefs and find the kitchen to be a fascinating place full of enticing smells, interesting equipment, and lots of activity. Everybody spends time in the kitchen, cooking, cleaning up, putting away groceries, or eating together, and toddlers like to be there, too. Cooking together gives them a chance to be part of the action and to make food for the whole family to enjoy. They also get to master new skills, try new foods, follow a sequence, and discover how things are made. It's all very exciting.

Experience is the best way to learn, even if the final product isn't perfect. Not every recipe will come out the way it's intended to. Cutting butter, kneading dough, grating cheese, cracking eggs, pouring milk, and stirring batter provide hands-on activity that is engaging and fun for two-year-olds.

Take time to enjoy what you are doing. Encourage your child to use his hands and do as much of the preparation as possible. Let him

feel the texture of flour and the grains of sugar with his fingers. Smell the different spices and watch what happens when you mix dry and wet ingredients together. Put your blender and food processor aside and chop, stir, and mix by hand—remember that for your child all of these experiences are new.

Make sure your cooking equipment is safe and easy to use. Metal bowls, plastic measuring cups, wooden spoons, and nonserrated butter knives are all very manageable for young children. When cooking together, don't use complicated equipment that your child can't handle.

For an extra good time, wear a special apron. You may even want to make a chef's hat together before you begin. And don't forget to put aside a special sponge for your child to help you with cleaning up.

Safety comes first. Let your child know that you alone are in charge of the stove. Never use sharp knives. Prepare ingredients that require cutting with sharp knives in advance. Avoid using glass containers or tools with breakable parts. Substitute plastic or disposable aluminum pans whenever possible.

Washing hands with soap is an important part of getting ready to cook. So soap up together as the first step in being a real chef.

Try these recipes, and add your own. Enjoy being chefs together, and the great enthusiasm that young children bring to cooking.

*PIZZA

Pizza is a favorite food for many families and is fun to make. Children especially enjoy working with the dough and learning how to make their own. With this recipe, you can make a special, small pizza with your child.

Ready-made pizza dough (available at grocery store or local pizza restaurant)
½ plastic cup tomato sauce
½ tsp. oregano
½ lb. shredded mozzarella cheese
½ cup grated parmesan cheese
cornmeal
olive oil
chopped vegetables, including onion, green or red peppers, mushrooms, broccoli, or spinach

1. Preheat oven to 425° F.

2. Together, grate the parmesan cheese, chop the vegetables, and cut the mozzarella. Set them aside while you prepare the dough.

3. Your child can bang, stretch, pound, and knead the dough. Use a rolling pin

to flatten it out. Your pizza doesn't have to be exactly round. Watch the elasticity of pizza dough as it stretches and contracts.

4. Give your child a little cornmeal to sprinkle on a piece of aluminum foil (using foil instead of a baking dish minimizes the mess). Place the dough on the foil.

5. "Paint" the dough with olive oil.

6. Spoon the tomato sauce onto the dough.

7. Shake oregano on the sauce.

8. Spread the cheeses and vegetables on top.

9. Bake for 20 to 25 minutes.

*BROCCOLI CHEESE CASSEROLE

Fresh or frozen, broccoli is a favorite vegetable for many children. Here's a way to mix it with cheese in a tasty casserole the whole family can enjoy for dinner.

3 cups chopped broccoli, cooked fresh or frozen spears

½ cup grated cheddar cheese

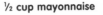

½ cup mayonnaise

½ can condensed cream of mushroom soup

5–6 Saltine crackers

1 egg

1. Preheat oven to 375° F.

2. Combine all ingredients in a bowl. Mix well.

3. Grease an individual aluminum loaf pan by rubbing a paper towel with a little oil on it. Pour in mixture.

4. Place 5 to 6 Saltine crackers in a zip-lock plastic bag. Your child can crumble them by squeezing or pounding the bag.

5. Open the bag and pour the coarsely-crumbled crackers on top of the broccoli mixture.

6. Bake for about 30 minutes until casserole is firm and lightly brown.

*THUMBPRINT JELLY COOKIES

Easy to make and delicious to eat, children love making their thumbprints in each and every cookie. Halve the recipe to make a smaller batch of cookies.

> Take a trip to the supermarket to begin your cooking. Buy the ingredients together and imagine how delicious they will be. It's fun to find the butter, the flour, the eggs, the zucchini, and apples each in their own special places.

1 egg yolk

½ cup confectioners' sugar

2 cups flour

½ lb. butter

Jelly

1. Preheat oven to 350° F.

2. Mix all ingredients except jelly and form into a big ball.

3. Break off small, meatball-sized pieces.

4. Your child can flatten each ball with the palm of her hand. Then use a fork to print a design in each cookie.

5. Ask your child to show you her thumb by sticking it in the air. Then push it into the center of each cookie.

6. Fill each center with jelly.

7. Bake for about 20 minutes. Cool before eating.

Keep your eyes open for child-sized rolling pins. A handy alternative is the one inch cylinder from a set of wooden building blocks. These blocks also work well with play dough.

* BANANA CAKE

There's nothing like a warm piece of fresh banana cake for a delicious breakfast. Breaking eggs, mashing, pouring, stirring—this recipe has it all!

1 ripe banana

¼ cup margarine

1 egg

¼ cup vanilla yogurt

¾ cup flour

¼ cup sugar

½ tsp. baking powder

½ tsp. baking soda

½ tsp. vanilla

¼ tsp. cinnamon

1. With the peel still on, let your child squeeze the banana until it is soft. Remove the peel and mush the banana in a bowl.

2. Add the margarine and continue mixing.

3. Add the yogurt and stir.

4. Help your child break the egg and mix it in.

5. Add the flour and mix.

6. Add the sugar and mix.

7. Add the baking powder and baking soda and mix.

8. Add the vanilla. Encourage your child to smell it.

9. Shake in the cinnamon, enjoying its aroma as well.

10. Grease an individual aluminum loaf pan using a paper towel with a little oil on it.

11. Pour in the batter.

12. Bake in 325° F oven for one hour and fifteen minutes.

> Two-year-olds love to explore the taste, texture, and smell of ingredients. Tasting along the way is part of the fun. Avoid tasting anything with raw egg in it.

*PRETZELS (AND OTHER SHAPES)

Here's the ultimate hands-on recipe, with dough to knead, pull, stretch, squeeze, and roll until it's time to bake. Make tasty soft pretzels or use the dough to create snakes, shapes, or initials. Don't be surprised if your child doesn't want to stop to put his pretzels in the oven.

1 package dry yeast

¾ cup warm water

1 tbsp. sugar

pinch of kosher salt

1 cup whole wheat flour

1 cup unbleached white flour

1 egg

1. Preheat oven to 425° F.

2. Mix the yeast and water together for five minutes before you're ready to begin.

3. Pour white and whole wheat flour into a bowl and mix together with fingers.

4. Add sugar and mix.

5. Add a pinch of kosher salt to the bowl and mix.

6. Add the warm water/yeast mixture to form a ball.

7. Generously sprinkle flour on the table or on a cutting board. Place the dough on it and roll it with a rolling pin for about 5 minutes.

8. Roll the dough into coils to form pretzels or create your own shapes.

9. Brush the dough with the beaten egg.

10. Sprinkle with kosher salt.

11. Bake for 12 to 15 minutes, until golden brown.

*FRUIT KABOBS

This delicious, healthy snack is fun to make. Prepare extra fruit for tasting as you work. Fresh fruit is irresistible.

Fruit that can be cut into pieces or chunks: apples, pineapples, bananas, strawberries

Kabob sticks (cut off sharp end) or plastic coffee stirrers

1. Cut fruit into pieces.

2. Push each piece onto a stick.

3. Make one or two for a snack, or a trayful for a novel dessert.

*RED, WHITE, AND BLUE PARFAIT

Here's the perfect dish for the Fourth of July or any time you want something refreshing and nutritious to eat. Use it as a snack, a dessert, breakfast, or lunch.

Vanilla yogurt
Blueberries
Strawberries
Clear plastic cups

1. Slice the strawberries.
2. Place a few spoonfuls of yogurt into a cup.
3. Add a layer of strawberry slices, followed by a layer of yogurt.
4. Then a layer of blueberries and repeat to the top.

*RICE CAKE FACES

Keep these ingredients on hand and you'll always have a great snack to make. Try this recipe when a friend is visiting for added fun.

Rice cakes
Peanut butter or cream cheese
Jelly
Pieces of fruits or vegetables

1. Spread a rice cake with either peanut butter or cream cheese. A butter knife or tongue depressor is a handy—and safe—spreader.

2. Design a face—jelly hair, banana eyes, strawberry nose, apple mouth, or whatever your creativity and ingredients lead you and your child to do.

> Wooden tongue depressors are ideal for little hands that want to spread peanut butter on crackers. They are available at pharmacies and craft stores. Keep a supply on hand.

*ANTS ON A LOG

This traditional snack will remain a quick favorite for many years to come.

Celery cut into four-inch-long pieces
Cream cheese or peanut butter
Raisins

1. Spoon cream cheese or peanut butter into the center of the celery.
2. Add raisins along the center of the "log."

*SALAD TO GO

Here's an idea for a quick lunch or snack that you can eat right out of your hands.

Flat-bottomed ice-cream cones
Small pieces of lettuce
Cottage cheese
Crushed pineapple (or other small fruit)

1. Put a few pieces of lettuce in the bottom of an ice-cream cone.

2. Add a scoop of cottage cheese.

3. Top with crushed pineapple or other small fruit, and try variations with your favorite fruits and vegetables.

*APPLE BREAD PUDDING

Tearing bread, beating eggs, pouring milk, and enjoying the aroma of cinnamon and vanilla—this pudding is great to make together. It's delicious when warm right from the oven, or when eaten later in the day. Try it for breakfast.

4 beaten eggs

2 cups milk

⅓ cup sugar

½ tsp. ground cinnamon

½ tsp. vanilla

3 cups (4 slices) dry
   bread cubes

⅓ cup raisins (optional)

1 apple, chopped

1. In a mixing bowl, beat together eggs, milk, sugar, cinnamon, and vanilla.

2. Place dry bread cubes in a small round baking dish.

3. Sprinkle raisins and apples over bread.

4. Pour egg mixture over all.

5. Bake in a 325° F oven for 45 minutes, or until a knife inserted near the center comes out clean.

6. Serve warm or cool.

*THANKSGIVING STUFFING

Children love to be part of the Thanksgiving preparations. Tearing the bread for stuffing is a perfect job for them. But you don't have to wait until Thanksgiving to make this.

8" x 8" pan

1 loaf day old Italian bread

4 small apples, chopped

4 large mushrooms, chopped

1 small bunch parsley, chopped

2 stalks celery, chopped

1 stick margarine or butter

½ tsp. poultry seasoning

2 eggs

optional: green pepper (chopped), fresh peas, onions (chopped), nuts

1. Tear apart bread in large bowl.

2. Add apples, parsley, mushrooms, celery, and spices. Mix well.

3. Moisten with margarine and eggs.

4. Bake in 350° F oven for 30 minutes.

Sometimes it's helpful to pre-measure ingredients so that they are ready to use and more easily handled by small hands. Paper cups are practical for holding these ingredients.

*CHEESE PASTRIES

Get your hands and rolling pins ready to go. Enjoy these pastries when they're still warm and fresh out of the oven.

1 cup flour

¼ cup butter

½ cup (2 oz.) shredded cheese (Muenster, cheddar, any kind)

Spices, to taste (seasoned salt, garlic powder, paprika, etc.)

Cold water

1. Mix flour and butter together.

2. Add cheese, spice, and 1 tablespoon of water, and mix. Hands work best for mixing.

3. Continue to add water a little at a time until dough sticks together but is not soggy. Add flour if dough becomes sticky.

4. Roll out to ½" thickness, and cut into strips or make coil rolls with your hands.

5. Place on greased cookie sheet.

6. Bake at 350° F for 15 minutes or until browned and crispy.

step one tap tap tap

step two

Children need help learning how to crack an egg. Show your child how to give the egg three taps on the side of the bowl, the last tap being the hard one. Show her how to put both thumbs in the crack and pull apart the two halves of the shell so the egg slides out. It takes practice! And don't forget to hold the egg over the bowl.

Sing Along

Keep on singing! Try "Down by the Station" when you play train, and "The More We Get Together" when friends come to play.

*LITTLE RED CABOOSE

Little red caboose, chug, chug, chug

Little red caboose, chug, chug, chug

Little red caboose, behind the train,
    train, train, train

Smokestack on his back, back, back, back

Chugging down the track, track, track, track

Little red caboose behind the train.

*HELLO SONG (TO THE TUNE OF "ARE YOU SLEEPING")

Hello (child's name)

Hello (adult's name)

How are you? How are you?

We are glad to see you. We are glad to see you.

Wave goodbye. Wave goodbye.

*THE MORE WE GET TOGETHER

The more we get together, together, together

The more we get together, the happier we'll be

'Cause your friends are my friends

And my friends are your friends

The more we get together, the happier we'll be.

*MONKEY SEE

Monkey see, monkey do

Monkey does the same as you

We're going to clap, clap our hands

We're going to clap, clap our hands

We're going to jump, jump around . . . (etc.)

We're going to stomp, stomp our feet . . . (etc.)

*THE BEAR WENT OVER THE MOUNTAIN

The bear went over the mountain

The bear went over the mountain

The bear went over the mountain

To see what he could see

But all that he could see

But all that he could see

Was just another mountain

Was just another mountain

Was just another mountain

That's all that he could see

*DOWN BY THE STATION

Down by the station early in the morning

See the little puffer bellies all in a row

See the station master pull the little handle

Chug chug, choo choo, here we go!

*THE DRESSING SONG

Look at (child's name),

she's wearing a red shirt.

Look at (child's name),

she's wearing a red shirt.

Look at (child's name),

she's wearing a red shirt.

What a way to start the day!

*OLD MACDONALD

Old MacDonald had a farm,

E–I–E–I–O.

And on this farm he had some chicks,

E–I–E–I–O.

With a cheep, cheep here,

And a cheep, cheep there,

Here a cheep, there a cheep,

Everywhere a cheep, cheep.

Old MacDonald had a farm,

E–I–E–I–O.

Ducks . . . Quack

Sheep . . . Baa

Horse . . . Neigh

Cow . . . Moo

*POP! GOES THE WEASEL

All around the cobbler's bench

The monkey chased the weasel.

The monkey said it was all in fun.

Pop! Goes the weasel!

*WHERE IS THUMBKIN?

Where is Thumbkin?

Where is Thumbkin?

Here I am.

Here I am.

How are you this morning?

Very well, I thank you.

Run away, run away.

(Continue with Pointer, Middle Finger,

Ring Finger, and Pinkie.)

cheep cheep

92

Much bigger!

Moving Up in the World

Three-Year-Olds

Moving Up in the World
Three-Year-Olds

Three-year-olds love to hear about when they were little and are impressed with how grown up they are. They can engage in elaborate conversations, have strong opinions, and tell you in great detail what they think. They can be excellent reporters at this age and will give you a great deal of information with some accuracy, although they may not fully understand what they're saying. They have learned a lot in their three years of life, and it's a delight to be with them.

Three-year-olds can be an active part of a community. Many three-year-olds participate in preschool nursery or day-care programs. They are ready to enjoy collaborative play, to play tea party, or to make a train with other children. This type of activity, rich in fantasy and detail, helps children get along together, share their ideas, and understand the workings of the world.

Your three-year-old's increasing knowledge and greater emotional maturity make it possible for them to understand more complex sequences, to have a sense of time, and to understand cause and effect. She is ready for more complicated activities and is learning to be patient—she can follow the steps of a recipe with you, wait for glue to dry so a wood project can be painted, and can take turns in a simple board game. He has a longer attention span than ever and can listen to longer stories and sustain activities over time. And three-year-olds like new adventures and new places, as long as they know that they will return to the comfort and security of home.

Three-year-olds are capable artists, chefs, scientists, actors, and actresses. In this chapter, you will find the activity for whatever your child wants to be at the moment. They'll make whimsical necklaces, paper bag costumes, telescopes, herb terrariums, creature collages, and spice soup. Get ready to have a great time!

Art Smarts Plus

Your child is the artist, with his own vision and perspective. Set the stage with materials and a place to work, and let his imagination and whimsy take over.

*WHIMSICAL NECKLACES

Big, little, big. Big, little, big. Two red, one blue, two red, one blue. Three-year-olds begin to notice patterns around them and will enjoy creating their own patterns in their artwork. You can make whimsical necklaces from pasta, cut-up straws, dry cereal, pretzels, pieces of paper punched with holes, or whatever strikes your fancy. Shoelaces, yarn with a taped end for easy stringing, or heavy duty string are easiest for small hands to manage. Create your own pattern—two pastas, one straw, one pretzel, two pastas, one straw, one pretzel. Some children fill the entire string, and others prefer the lighter look of a few pieces. It's your child's whimsy that counts.

> Store materials that are unsafe for children to use alone in a safe place. These include scissors, staplers, pipe cleaners, and tape dispensers. Be sure to use only non-toxic glue, paint, crayons and markers.

*PLAYFUL PATTERNS

Be inventive and look around you for patterns when you do art together. Patterns can be part of many projects. Collage materials, paper strips, cut-out shapes, tissue paper, and paints, markers, and crayons can all be arranged in your child's own original patterns. For instance, glue a pattern collage—one piece of fabric, one piece of paper, fabric, paper, and so on. Create a color pattern—one dab of red paint, three dabs of blue, one dab of red paint, three dabs of blue. Singing along as your pattern emerges adds fun and spirit to the project.

*ONE-COLOR PICTURES

Make a "red picture," using only red things. Preschoolers love hunting and finding the right color materials. Use crayons, markers, paint, stickers, magazine pictures, pieces of construction paper, fabric, and buttons. Fill your wall with pictures of every color and make a rainbow wall!

*ONE-SHAPE PICTURES

As your child learns to identify simple shapes, choose one to make a shape picture. Cut shapes from construction paper, fabric, and old wrapping paper to use in your shapely art.

*STRIPE PICTURES

Stripes are all around us—on shirts, on flags, on wallpaper, and peppermint sticks. Make your own stripes by cutting out one- to two-inch wide strips of construction paper. Glue them onto a differently colored piece, leaving space in between to create the stripes. Or, make several differently colored stripes and arrange them in a repeating pattern. Try decorating all the blue stripes one way and the green stripes another.

*SAND ART

You can buy small bags of colored sand at your local aquarium or pet store. Drip glue onto a piece of heavy paper or cardboard in a random design. Sprinkle sand—either with your fingers or in a shaker— onto the glue. Shake off the excess. Old spice jars work well as shakers for this activity.

*FRUIT CONTAINER BOXES

The plastic containers from strawberries or blueberries can become great boxes for storing special possessions. Glue on feathers, pompoms, ribbons, or paper—any collage materials will do. You'll have the fanciest fruit boxes on the block!

Cardboard and plastic fruit trays from the supermarket are handy surfaces for collages.

*FRUIT BOX COLLAGES

Ask your local grocer to give you the large molded paper holders that apples are shipped in. They look almost like giant egg cartons, and they're great for collages. Your child can fill each compartment with an assortment of materials, or you can cut them up to use in several projects.

*TEXTURE COLLAGES

Bumpy, smooth, scratchy, soft—use your fingers to find textured objects for a collage that you can feel together. Try cottonballs, sandpaper, velvet, corduroy, corrugated cardboard, sponges, or feathers. You'l love "seeing" your art with your fingers!

Some children add layer upon layer to a collage. Others are finished after gluing two buttons to a piece of cardboard. You'll get to know your child's style over time. Respect individual differences and interests.

*TORN PAPER COLLAGES

Tearing paper looks easy, but it takes practice to get both of your hands moving in opposite directions. Help your child to tear pieces of light-weight paper. Rip off different size pieces to glue in a collage. Uneven edges give it an interesting look. Experiment with different colors and types of paper.

*CREATURE COLLAGES

Draw a strangely-shaped creature and cut it out. Your child can name it and give it as many eyes, hands, feet, noses as she wants. Make it one or many colors. Three-year-olds have terrific senses of humor and will appreciate the silliness of a four-eyed green and purple polka dot monkey cat with six legs—so will you!

*TELESCOPES

Decorate a paper towel roll to use as a telescope. Tape a piece of cellophane or plastic wrap to each end to create a lens. Experiment with different colors of cellophane or plastic wrap to see the world in a new way.

Accept your child's view of the world. Hair can be green, eyes can be purple, and buildings can be smaller than people.

*FIREHOSES

Paper towel rolls or wrapping paper rolls make great pretend firehoses. Paint one red—or decorate it however your child likes—and pretend he's a firefighter.

*POCKETS AND POUCHES

Children like pockets, and you can make one easily out of two paper plates. Cut one plate in half and staple it to the bottom half of the other plate. Tape over the staples with masking tape. Your child can decorate it. Punch a hole in the top, put a piece of yarn through it, and hang it on a doorknob or on a belt to wear.

Your child will know what to put in it—a favorite stone, an old drawing, play money, or a small toy. You'll be surprised to see what disappears into your child's pockets and pouches!

*SCULPTURES

Use cardboard as a foundation, and your child can construct a sculpture with paper towel or toilet paper rolls. Cut them into different sizes, glue them, and decorate them. Add them to your growing "At-Home" Art Museum.

*PICTURE FRAMES

There are many ways to make great picture frames. Cardboard cartons provide sturdy material if you take them apart and cut out a shape in which to insert a picture.

Popsicle sticks or tongue depressors glued together in a square also work well. For these frames, glue the picture on the back of the frame. Paper plates, or paper fruit trays from the supermarket can have a picture glued directly on the front.

All of these frames provide wonderful surfaces for decoration before you insert the picture. For a three-dimensional look, glue on buttons, pebbles, small seashells, or pasta. These frames are terrific for family snapshots as well as your child's own artwork.

*GREETING CARDS

Your child can easily make her own greeting cards. Fold a piece of construction paper in half and cut out a shape on the front. Glue your child's photograph on the inside cover so that it shows through. Your child's decorations will make this uniquely hers.

*CLEAN-UP BOX

Make clean-up time more inviting with a collection of homemade boxes. Use shoe boxes or cardboard cartons and decorate the boxes with pictures of what will go in each one.

Everyday sorting and classifying is an important part of life for a three-year-old, and making special boxes encourages your child to be more personally interested in clean-up time.

*PAPER BAG HATS

Take a medium-size paper bag and fold the top over into a cuff. Decorate it with crayons, markers, and stickers. Attach colorful paper or ribbon streamers, or stick pipe cleaners through the top to liven it up.

Turn large brown paper bags from the supermarket into wonderful helmets. Trim several inches off the open end of the bag, then cut out a large circle for your child's face. These are easy to make when friends come to visit.

*PAPER BAG PUPPETS

Lunch-size brown paper bags can become hand puppets with a little imagination and a lot of glue. Keep the bag folded, with the rectangular bottom facing up and the open end of the bag toward you. Create a face on the rectangular bottom with buttons, yarn, fabric scraps, paper, and markers. Decorate the bottom part of the bag as the puppet's body. Once it dries, bring your puppet to life by inserting your hand so your fingers curl inside the puppet's face. Save your puppets as your cast of characters grows.

Three-year-olds have their own ideas about which materials they prefer. Provide them with the opportunity to make their own choices.

*SEWING CARDS

Have your child choose a large picture that your child really likes from a magazine. Cut it out and glue it to a piece of lightweight cardboard. Punch several holes around the edge of the picture. Your child can "sew" it with a shoelace or yarn.

*LIFE-SIZE PAPER CHILDREN

Young children find life-size models of themselves very appealing. Large sheets of heavy brown wrapping paper work best for this project. Spread out the paper. As your child lays on the paper, trace the outline of his body. Cut it out, talking about the different parts of his body.

Choose materials to make a face, hair, and clothing. Sometimes children like to copy what they are wearing at that moment. When you're done, find a great place to display your "paper friends."

*LIFE-SIZE PAPER DOLLS

Double large brown wrapping paper to make two outlines of your child's body at the same time. After decorating them, staple the two pieces together around the edges, leaving several openings. Stuff it with crumpled newspaper or tissue paper and finish stapling. Keep these paper playmates around the house. Set them in corners, prop them on a shelf, dance with them, and enjoy their lively and colorful presence!

*WOOD SCULPTURES

You can buy a bag of pre-cut, pre-sanded wood shapes at a crafts store. When your child glues them together on a cardboard base, these random wooden shapes create fabulous three-dimensional sculptures. After the glue dries, add paint or glue on whatever strikes your child's fancy.

*STICKER HOUSES

Cut out a simple house from construction paper and decorate it with colored shape stickers. As you work together, talk about your home or the building. What kind of noise does the doorbell make? What can you see when you look out the window? What rooms are in your building? Is there an upstairs or downstairs? Is there a front door, a back door, an elevator, or a staircase? Put several together and make your own town grow.

Tape over staples and the exposed ends of pipe cleaners to avoid scratches. Masking tape works well.

*PLASTIC BAG BOOKS

These easy-to-read books are fun to make. Let your child choose a theme—cars, food, colors, animals—and look through magazines and catalogs together for pictures. Cut paper to fit inside zip-lock bags. Glue the pictures on the pre-cut paper and place one page in each bag. Turn your bags into a book by stapling the bags together or by punching two holes in each bag and tying them together with a piece of yarn. Change your book or add to it when a fresh idea comes your way. Watch your library of homemade books grow.

*PAINTING WITH STRING

String is another great painting tool. Dip a piece of string in paint and drag it across a piece of paper. Watch the designs it makes and experiment together. No brush clean-up today!

*IVORY SNOW AND WATER

Mix together Ivory Snow laundry powder and water until it becomes the consistency of paste, and add a drop of food coloring. Your child will enjoy squishing this mixture around with her fingers on a piece of heavy paper or on a large cookie sheet. Keep water available for easy clean-up. Get your hands messy with soap!

*MAKE AN OUTDOOR SCENE

This project combines several steps to create a familiar scene from outdoors. First paint a background on a large piece of paper. (Glue several small pieces of paper together if you don't have large paper on hand.) Stick to the basics at first—green for grass, blue for sky or sea, and brown for the earth.

Talk together about what you see in each of these settings and decide what will be in your scene—trees, fish, stars, flowers, or animals. Adults can cut out the shapes, and children can design them with paint, collage materials, and glue. Put it all together and bring the outdoors inside!

*STAINED GLASS

Cut shapes out of colored tissue paper. Place them on a piece of clear contact paper that you've cut in an interesting shape and size. Overlap different colors of tissue paper to make new colors. When you're finished, cover the entire collage with another piece of clear contact paper. Punch a hole in the top and string a piece of yarn through it. Place it in the window for a beautiful stained-glass hanging.

*SIDEWALK CHALK

Sidewalks are great surfaces for drawing with chalk. You can start out with white chalk and advance to different colors as your child gets older. Chalk washes off the sidewalk easily.

Imagine That!

Three-year-olds pretend all day long—at home, in the car, at breakfast, alone, or with friends. Play along with them and enjoy being invited to their imaginary world.

*PAPER BAG COSTUMES

You can make simple costumes with paper bags from the supermarket, turned upside down. Cut a hole on top for the head and one on each side for arms. Add a scarf for a belt, and a hat or helmet you've made, and your child is ready to slay a dragon.

*PILLOWCASE COSTUMES

Old pillowcases become costumes easily, so keep some on hand. Cut a hole in the top to fit over your child's head and cut holes on both sides for her arms. Glue on fabric scraps or trimmings for decoration. These versatile costumes can last for years.

*BOX FURNITURE

Smaller cardboard boxes can become hot stoves with red construction paper burners and magic marker or pipe cleaner handles. Cover a box with a towel for a tea party table or line it with a blanket for a doll bed.

*BOX HOUSE

If you're lucky enough to come across a discarded box from a refrigerator, grab it! Your child now has a private house, and will enjoy moving in. Cut out windows, a door, and maybe even a sunroof for ventilation. Use old bathroom rugs or towels as carpets. Move in a few favorite toys, stuffed animals, and a comfortable pillow. The box can also become a spaceship, a train, an ocean liner, a castle, or anything else you and your child imagine.

*BOX CAR

Children love to sit in large cardboard boxes, and you can turn one into a car—or any other vehicle—by cutting out a door and using paper plates for a steering wheel and tires. Draw a dashboard with magic markers. Add a pillow for a seat cushion and have a great trip. Put on your sunglasses so you can see the road!

*TENTS

Create a cozy, private indoor tent by draping a sheet over a table to enclose a child-size space. These "tents" are great fun to play in together with a friend.

*ELEVATOR GOING UP!

Step into your own private elevator for a new round of fun. Spread a large towel on the floor to make your elevator and step right in. Push the pretend button.

"The door is opening." (demonstrate with your hands),

"We're getting on the elevator." (step onto the sheet)

"We're pushing two." (push button)

"We're going up." (look up)

"We're on the second floor. Everyone out." (step off the sheet).

At each floor, look around, describe what you see, and step out. For example, "We're on the flying floor." Everybody flies around before stepping back into the elevator to ride to the next floor. Stop at the bouncing, jumping, whispering, even the ice-cream cone floor. And don't forget the lion and tiger floor. Bring your dramatic flair, sound effects and all, into the elevator with you. Elevator going up—step right in!

*IMAGINARY BALLOONS

Here's a great game to play when a few friends come to visit. It works especially well with three or more children. Get in a small, tight circle, or stand facing your child if it's just the two of you. Say, "Let's blow up a balloon." Your child decides what color balloon to blow up. "We're blowing up a (color) balloon." Pretend you're blowing and blowing, stepping back to move the circle out wider with each blow. Keep blowing until "Pop!" the balloon explodes, and everyone falls down!

*PLUGLIK SOUP

Even though you can't eat it, Pluglik soup is great fun to make when playing outdoors. Give your child a large pot with a bit of water, and a big wooden spoon. Add special ingredients— pebbles, grass, a few leaves, small twigs, and dirt. Mix well, adding water as needed.

Serve outdoors for a Pluglik party. Use toy dishes, invite a few friends, and ask them to bring their favorite stuffed animal—Pluglik soup is known to be a favorite of many stuffed animals.

*PACKING A SUITCASE

Using a favorite small tote, overnight bag, or backpack, your child can pack to "take a trip." He can pack whatever he thinks he'll need—socks, toothbrush, pajamas, a teddy bear. Take this bag to a pretend destination. Make sure you know what's inside. If you don't, you may not be able to find it for a while.

Homemade Instruments

*DRUM

Save a large cylindrical oatmeal box and its plastic lid. Cut a piece of contact paper to fit around the box. With the backing still on the contact paper, decorate the front with stickers, markers and paper, and flat collage materials. Then peel off the backing, and attach the decorated contact paper around the oatmeal box. You've got a perfect child-size drum! Let your fingers be the drumsticks.

*SHAKERS

Plastic yogurt containers with firmly-fitted tops make great musical shakers. Fill them with a handful of dried beans, rice, buttons, or pebbles. Make sure you secure the top with glue as well as tape. Decorate as you're inspired.

Metal candy tins two to four inches in diameter, with tops and bottoms that fit snugly together also make great shakers with a different sound.

*TAMBOURINE

Turn two paper plates into a tambourine by stapling them together around the edge and filling them with a few dried beans. Be sure to tape the edge to cover the staples completely. Decorate and get your fingers tapping!

More Kids in the Kitchen

What was new at two becomes even more exciting and fun at three. Three-year-olds know what cooking is all about and look forward to pouring milk, cracking eggs, mixing in a large bowl, and kneading dough. They love sharing their creations with the family and take great pride in serving the pizza they made for dinner. You may be lucky enough to be invited to their "restaurant," with freshly baked cookies on the menu.

For a selection of great recipes that work well for young children, look back to the cooking section on page 82. Begin them at two, at three, or whenever you're ready to cook with your child. Find your favorites and make them part of your family's good food repertoire.

For a really terrific time, combine your three-year-old's pleasure in cooking with his great flair for make-believe. Include him as you cook, working next to each other.

Keep a magnifying glass on hand for a closer look. Add a small one to your "Explorer Bag."

to know "Why?" Doing these activities with your child is a great beginning.

*SPICE SOUP

Here's a great recipe for "Spice Soup"—to make, **but not to eat!**

Give your child his own large bowl and mixing spoon while you're making a meal. Pass him the odds and ends of whatever you are preparing— carrot tops, onion peels, celery leaves, apple cores, or a few pieces of pasta. Add water. Stir and shake in a few old spices which you've set aside for your child to use. Keep stirring. Keep adding. "Spice Soup," although not edible, is great fun for your child to make while working along next to you.

Hands-On Science

Full of questions and ready for answers, three-year-olds make great scientists, eager to explore, observe, collect, put together, and take apart. They want

*EXPLORER BAGS

Take a large plastic zip-lock bag, punch holes on both sides, and string it with a piece of brightly-colored yarn to make a shoulder strap. Decorate the bag with stickers and label it "Explorer Bag."

Off you go exploring! Look around with your child and collect things that are interesting— twigs, flowers, rocks, leaves, and even a single blade of grass.

*EXPLORER SONG

Get your child into the spirit of exploring with this song (to the tune of "This Old Man"):

> Let's explore, let's explore
> Step right in, open up the door
> Look and listen, touch things too
> How does it work and what does it do?

*ROCK AND SHELL PAINTING

Large rocks and shells you find as you explore make interesting surfaces for painting and gluing. Bring a few extra home with you from your excursions.

*ROCK CREATURES

Make rock creatures by gluing various size rocks together and adding feathers, eyes, pipe cleaners, and fabric. (To glue rocks together, use glue generously and hold the rocks in place until the glue begins to set.) Start your own creature collection.

*LEAF PICTURES

A trip outside to the backyard or park is great for collecting leaves. Bring home what you find. Add paper and glue for a picture that brings nature indoors. At different times of the year, your leaf picture will have a new look, just like in nature.

*PLANTING

Fill a clear plastic cup with soil. Sprinkle in some marigold or radish seeds, and add a little water every day. The seeds will start to sprout in a day or two. It doesn't take long to see results.

*HERB TERRARIUMS

Turn a two-liter plastic soda bottle into an herb terrarium. Cut the bottle into two parts, leaving the bottom about three inches deep. Line the bottom with two inches of soil and plant some herb seeds—parsley or chives work well. Tape the two pieces of the bottle back together with clear plastic tape and watch what grows. Keep the bottle top on, taking it off only to water the seeds as needed. When your seeds have grown into herbs, use them to season your food as you cook together!

*GREENHOUSE TERRARIUMS

Get a large, clear plastic water or soda bottle. Spread glue down the length of one side to prevent it from rolling. When the glue dries, lay the bottle on its side, glue facing downward.

Make a small opening in the top and add a few inches of dirt. After an exploring trip, add rocks, moss, leaves, or anything else you have collected in your bag. Water as needed. Over time, watch the water evaporate and drip down, creating a greenhouse effect.

*RAINMAKERS

Use a sponge and water to demonstrate how it rains. Holding a sponge in the air over a large bowl, slowly pour a little water into a dry sponge. Watch it expand like a growing rain cloud. As the sponge fills up, water comes through, and it starts to rain!

*SEEDS

Seeds don't naturally come in a package. Your child sees them all the time. Start collecting the seeds from the foods you eat. Include orange, apple, grapefruit, and watermelon seeds. Save some peach, plum, avocado, and cherry pits.

Observe them over time, looking for changes. Open some up. Glue some on paper for a seed picture. Try sprouting dried lima beans by placing them on a folded paper towel and moistening them daily.

*FLOWERS INSIDE AND OUT

You can learn a lot about something by taking it apart and seeing how it is made. Collect a few flowers from outdoors or buy some at the flower store. Look at them together. Feel the different textures—stems, leaves, petals. Take a flower apart gently so you can see each part. Look at several kinds of flowers. Squish a whole flower in your hands to feel how much moisture is inside.

*PAPER FLOWERS

Glue a twig to a piece of paper to use as a stem. Make roots out of pieces of yarn and flower petals out of ripped paper or crushed tissue paper. Add real or paper leaves. Glue some seeds to the center of the flower to make the flower more real.

*INSIDE/OUTSIDE HANDS

Here's a simple way to make a three-dimensional model of a hand to show what's inside.

Have your child begin by feeling the bones in her own hands. Trace an adult's hand on construction

> Science isn't always a project. It's all around you—ice cubes melting, puddles evaporating, skinned knees healing, fingernails growing, and steam rising from your tea kettle.

paper. Cut it out, and this becomes the bones of the hand you are constructing. Make a layer of muscles out of plasticine or play dough, stretching it over the hand. Talk about how soft and stretchy muscles are. Feel the muscles in your own hands.

Notice the veins in your hands and make them by placing pipe cleaners on top of the layer of muscles.

Your bones, muscles, and veins are covered with skin. Cover your model of a hand with "skin" by sliding it into a clear surgical glove that you buy in a drugstore. This activity is a great way for children to begin to understand what's inside them.

*BUGS

Go outside to go hunting and digging for bugs. Bugs that live on the ground like moist places. Look for leaves with pieces missing—evidence that hungry bugs may be around. Bugs often hide in dead leaves, about one inch underground or under rocks. Dig slowly.

It's also fun to pretend you are bugs—wiggle like worms, scrunch up like caterpillars, hop like grasshoppers. Create your own bugs by making three small balls out of newspaper. Glue or tape them together and attach pipe cleaner legs!

*APPLESAUCE COLORS

Mixing colors together to see new ones emerge is exciting. Mix food coloring with applesauce—start with blue, add yellow, and you've made green applesauce! Try it with red and blue to make purple, or red and yellow to make orange.

> Books add to your scientific repertoire. Many wonderful storybooks illustrate changes in nature and animal life. Remember to look at nonfiction books as well.

*OIL AND WATER DON'T MIX!

See what happens when you try to mix oil and water. Use a clear plastic jar with a lid that can be screwed on tightly. Pour in two to three inches of salad oil. Add a few drops of food coloring to water and pour a few inches of this solution into the jar. Watch what happens. Put on the lid tightly and shake the jar. What do you see? Let the solution settle and see how it ends up. Do it over and over, and watch what happens!

*THIRSTY CELERY

All living things need water to survive, and your child knows what it feels like to be thirsty. Demonstrate how celery "drinks" water. Stand a tall stalk of celery with the leaves still on in a solution of water and food coloring. Watch what happens over the next few days.

*FEEL BAG

Put a half dozen different items into a shopping bag. Choose items that are familiar to your child.

Your child reaches in, with her eyes closed, and pulls out one item. She can then identify it by what it feels like.

* SPACE HELMETS

Take a trip to outer space and see the world through different eyes. Turn a large brown grocery bag upside down. Cut out an oval the size of your child's face. Tape colored cellophane paper to fill the hole. As your child wears his "space helmet," he will see how the world looks through different "lenses." Make a few helmets, using different colors—it's fun to compare how things look.

Moving Ahead . . .

We hope you've had many good times using the ideas and activities in WONDERPLAY. By now, your home is bursting with drums, egg carton treasure boxes, play dough sculptures, and secret hide-outs. Your child is developing new skills, talents, and interests and is ready to move out into the world of school and friends.

All that you've done up to now is the foundation for what comes next. Build on what you've learned, remembering to take a fresh look at old favorites. Take WONDERPLAY into the future as you have new, exciting adventures together.

Still growing!

Acknowledgments

The 92nd Street Y Parenting Center has always been a collaborative effort sustained by the knowledge, enthusiasm, professionalism, and energy of its excellent staff. WONDERPLAY is a reflection of this history and tradition, and would not have been possible without the contributions of many people.

For their constant help and good-natured support throughout the research and writing of this book, we would like to thank Barbara Katz and Gaby Greenberg. Their commitment to this project, their constructive comments, and their many suggestions have been invaluable.

The entire Parenting Center staff generously contributed hours of time to this work, sharing their experiences, expertise, and creativity. WONDERPLAY is filled with what our staff does so well every day with the parents and young children who come to the Parenting Center.

A heartfelt thanks to Margaret Joseph whose determination and careful research helped us immeasureably in bringing this project to completion. We also greatly appreciate Sylvia Avner's enthusiasm for bringing books into the lives of young children. A special thanks to Maxine Berger who helped us plan and shape this book. Lois Alter Mark has worked with us from the beginning, and we are grateful for her extensive contribution to our work, as well as for her positive encouragement all along the way.

We would also like to thank David Borgenicht, our editor at Running Press, for his enthusiastic appreciation of our work and his thoughtful suggestions for improvement. Working with him has been a rewarding experience.

Our families have lived with us through the many drafts and deadlines involved in the creation of this book. They have encouraged us when needed, sharpened our pencils, gotten us "on-line," and spared us for nights and weekends as we immersed ourselves in this project. We thank them for always being in our corner.

—**Fretta Reitzes and Beth Teitelman**

Index of Activities

For more creative activities to do with your child, ask your bookseller for BABY GAMES ($12.95, ISBN 0-87471-617-4), the childhood classic, also from Running Press.